BECOMING
TOXIC
PERSON
PROOF

SARAH K RAMSEY

ISBN: Hardback 978-1-64184-595-3
ISBN: Paperback 978-1-64184-596-0
ISBN: Ebook 978-1-64184-597-7

Published By LionHead Publishing

Dedicated to the Wondrous Women of
the past, present, and future.

CONTENTS

PART 1: GETTING CONTROL OF YOUR HEAD, YOUR HEART AND YOUR LIFE

PART 2: STRATEGIES FOR DEALING WITH THE TOXIC PEOPLE IN YOUR LIFE

ACKNOWLEDGEMENTS

I am grateful to everyone who made this book a reality starting with my very cute and very wonderful husband who graciously picked up meals and didn't complain about me writing instead of cooking, my parents who let me use my childhood bedroom to shut out the world and focus on putting words to the page, and my sweet children for giving me the motivation to create a better world for them and their future kids.

Thank you to my editor Elizabeth Lyon and my book design team at JetLaunch for working with my speedy deadlines. I am also forever grateful to James Wilson who has been the first person to see everything I have written over the years.

I'm thankful to all the men and women who allowed me to share their stories in this book and the team of Beta Team readers especially Beth Holmes who graciously took time out of their lives to make this dream a reality.

Of course, none of this would be possible without the tribe of humans who have picked me up when I am down and brought clarity to my own life. Thank you friends for the years in which you have watched me fall, watch me fail and watched me fly. I love and value you more than words can say.

PREFACE

This book isn't meant to declare that some people are "good" and others are "bad." This book is meant to suggest that some people are good for you to be around, and some people are bad for you to be around.

Let's first get clear about what we mean by toxic. I am not addressing someone's value as a human being; I'm addressing their ability to add value to or take away value from *your* human experience. Every human can have their own inherent worth; however, that does not mean that every human is worth giving time, energy, and resources.

You are likely to have people in your life who sometimes disrupt it as well as people who will have a long-term pattern of disruptive behavior. As we look into what it means to be toxic, please also remember that truly toxic behavior is a pattern. We all have bad days and bad moments, but most people do not exhibit long-term destructive patterns or a constant collection of destructive moments.

Toxic Behaviors May Include:

- Having one set of rules for themselves and a different set of rules for others.
- Having wants, needs, moods, and interests that always take priority over those of others.
- Needing it to always be their turn.
- Doing something nice for you or someone you care about in order to change your mind about something.

- Focusing on image management and being willing to do good things as long as it makes them look good.
- Behaving one way in public and another way in private.
- Avoiding responsibility.
- Using their anger or aggression to get their way and compel others to back down.
- Using your vulnerabilities against you to get their way.
- Getting you to do the work of the relationship.
- Being predictably unpredictable.
- Constantly needing others to bail them out of problems they create.
- Denying responsibility for their own life and the consequences of their own behaviors.
- Having a consistent pattern of lying and secrets.
- Being masters at "The Flip" and turning everything back on you. In fact, if you showed them this list, they could probably talk you into the notion that *you* are the toxic one.
- Always finding trouble. If they get bored, they may start trouble. As Hank Moody in "Californication" tells us, "I don't find trouble, trouble just finds me."[1] If they have a pattern of trouble, then they are trouble for you.
- Finding ways to significantly punish you when they don't get their way. You start to feel like you are getting trained. This is not your imagination. You are being trained.
- Making you feel small, wrong, overly responsible, and/or consistently confused.
- Turning things around so they always get away with things.
- Switching between being the know-it-all hero and the you-owe-me-this victim.

Toxic Behaviors Do NOT Include:

1. Needy sometimes.
2. Angry sometimes.
3. Having a bad day every once in a while.
4. Saying something they didn't mean.

5. Awkward to talk to.
6. Sometimes acting like they know it all.
7. Bossy sometimes.
8. Going through a hard time and needing to create space for themselves to heal, which could mean not being there for work or relationships in ways they have been in the past.
9. Annoying sometimes.
10. Negative sometimes.
11. Whiny sometimes.
12. Irritating sometimes.
13. Selfish sometimes
14. Dramatic sometimes.
15. Controlling sometimes. (Please notice the word sometimes.)
16. Avoiding things sometimes.
17. No sense of humor.
18. Not likable sometimes.
19. Someone who rubs you the wrong way sometimes.
20. Someone who doesn't do what you want.

Think about it this way: Imagine you pack your work fridge with your favorite sparkling water. A frustrating person may take your water or put their food in front of your water. A frustrating person may sip his own water so loudly that it distracts you from work.

A toxic person, on the other hand, is much more than just frustrating. A toxic person will play mind tricks on you to gain the upper hand. In fact, they might trick you into believing that the reason you were able to buy the water in the first place was because the toxic person was so wonderful! Or, the toxic person might consistently forget his or her water, spill their water, or pour their water on someone else and then expect you to give them all of *your* water. When you don't want to give them your water, they will make sure everyone at the office knows you are a horrible person for not doing so. They will perhaps convince everyone that you are not a team player and deserve to be fired. Then, to make the situation even more confusing, they might try to be nice to you and suggest that if you trade offices with them, they will make this all go away. Battle shocked, you will give them your office and then sign up for mental health sessions, trying to figure out what in the world happened and why they made such a big deal out of the water. You will find yourself feeling grateful toward the toxic person because he saved your job—and yet angry at the toxic person because you had to give up your office. You will be extremely confused and unsure of what just happened. You will not be able to figure out if you are a bad person for not giving him the water or if he is a bad person for asking for the water and causing such a scene. You will find yourself asking what is wrong with you and wondering if you can trust your own reality.

In this book, we will use the term "toxic person encounter" interchangeably with the term "toxic relationship." If your life has been negatively affected because of a coworker, friend, parent, partner, or loved one, then you have had a toxic person encounter. The term "toxic relationship" often has a romantic connotation. However, toxic person encounters do not only happen within romantic encounters, and toxic people damage people other than their lovers.

Some readers' toxic person encounters will have lasted ten weeks, while other readers will have dealt with a toxic person for ten years. This book will help both readers become Toxic Person Proof™ by helping them understand what type of person they are dealing with and helping them decide how to handle difficult personalities.

INTRO
DEFINING TOXIC PERSON PROOF™

"I have come to believe that caring for myself is not self-indulgent. Caring for myself is an act of survival."

—Audre Lorde

Have you ever participated in an ice breaker exercise where you were asked, "If you could choose a superpower, what would it be?" If you were a teenage boy, you may have chosen X-ray vision. If you were a mother with young kids, you probably chose to have an extra set of arms when needed. If you were climbing the ladder in your career, you possibly chose the ability to function without sleep. Maybe you wanted to predict the future (hello, stock market!) or fly like a bird or swim like a fish. Maybe you wanted to read minds.

I wanted to become Toxic Person Proof™.

I wanted to stop being taken advantage of, stop the habit of people pleasing, stop wasting my dreams on people who had no plans to change, and stop wasting my words on people who had no desire to listen. I wanted to feel safe in my own skin again, safe in my ability to read a situation, safe in my choices of who I hired and who I let watch my kids, safe in choosing whom I invited into my home and to whom I gave my time.

An individual who is Toxic Person Proof™:

1. Knows how to be kind without having your kindness used against you.
2. Has the emotional/social intelligence to move toward healthy people and away from unhealthy people.
3. Has the confidence to trust himself or herself.
4. Is able to intentionally control his or her own thoughts, even if someone else is trying to control them.
5. Has the ability to know herself, grow herself, and protect herself.

www.thevisualinfluence.com

If you want to have those abilities and become Toxic Person Proof™, congratulations! This book is about how to improve your life! The best time to read this book is before you ever experience pain and confusion because of a toxic person. The next best time to read this book is when you want to ensure you never experience the pain and confusion of a toxic person again. This book is for you if you want to learn to protect yourself and those you care about from being tricked, conned, taken advantage of, or fooled.

Fair warning: you are probably going to feel angry while reading sections of this book. You are probably going to get mad at the toxic people who have taken advantage of you and mad at yourself for not seeing the reality sooner. You might be mad at me for pointing out the things you don't want to see, and mad at yourself as the lightbulbs of the past turn on and the darkness fades away.

Becoming Toxic Person Proof™ is a journey for the brave. Or at least a journey for those who want to be brave! Get ready to confront deeply held thoughts that have served toxic people but haven't served you. Get ready to see how much parental training, religious training, academic training, or even psychological training has paved the way for toxic people to keep playing their games. Get ready to discover ways you have been vulnerable, and ways your strengths have been used against you. Get ready to gain back more time, money, and sleep as you stop wasting endless hours trying to figure things out with your therapist.

Perhaps obviously, I wanted to become Toxic Person Proof™ because I have not always *been* Toxic Person Proof™. (Insert blinking lights that read "Understatement of the year.")

Before starting this journey and having little-to-no understanding of who was most susceptible to toxic people, I couldn't comprehend how wonderful people could have their best qualities used against them. The little girl who is willing to help the teacher. The little boy who sticks up for a friend getting bullied. The young teen who's always checking in on her friends. The person who's committed to her faith. The person who's committed to his family. The employee who's committed to the company. The man trying his best to avoid failing at something. The woman trying her best not to rock the boat. The human trying to remain loyal and do right by others.

These are the people most often taken advantage of by toxic people. People who have had their kindness used against them, and who thought loving was the same as rescuing. People who thought humility was a virtue that entailed trusting everyone else more than they trusted themselves. People who were trying to do the right thing and got duped.

People like me. People like you.

I wrote this book because I want to stop seeing toxic people win. I want to stop hearing story after story of "I thought he was a good guy!" or "I just assumed that if I gave her one more chance, things would change" or "I thought something was weird, but I told myself I was just being judgmental and went ahead with the deal anyway." This book is designed to keep you safe! There are wonderful people out there, and there are toxic people out there. This book is designed to help you fill your life with healthy people and protect you from toxic people. We will explore the way that toxic behavior exists on a spectrum and get clear on exactly who in your life is toxic.

HOW TO KNOW IF YOUR SITUATION IS/ WAS TOXIC

"Was my relationship toxic?"

"Was my mother toxic?"

"Is my boss a narcissist or just a jerk?"

"Whose fault was it?"

"Why did they make me feel like I was the crazy one? No one else ever said that about me."

"Do you think they have a personality disorder?"

These are common questions asked by those who are concerned about being in (or having been in) a toxic relationship. Studying personality disorders that can be overlapped with addiction issues that can be overlapped with mental health issues that can be overlapped with infidelity that can be overlapped with trauma that can be overlapped with selfishness can be a bit confusing, to say the least. Even that sentence is confusing!

Taking an intense look at personality disorders is not the purpose of this book. The resources already available on this topic are nearly endless and include the areas of the Dark Triad, narcissism, sociopathy, psychopathy, borderline personality disorder, antisocial personality disorder, and addiction. Further, diagnosing toxic people is not the purpose of this book. My gift to you is not more research on toxic people! My gift to you is teaching you how to trust yourself, even if a toxic person is trying to confuse you.

Unfortunately, simply having information isn't enough to make you Toxic Person Proof™. People who have had toxic person encounters are both grateful and horrified when they learn about topics like gaslighting, personality disorder, and narcissism. They are grateful to have manipulation and power dynamics defined by experts, and horrified to realize toxic people do these things on purpose. Information is powerful, and having it is an amazing first step in being able to begin moving forward after a toxic person encounter. However, having information alone does not make you Toxic Person Proof™.

Imagine someone wrestling with a crocodile. There they are, in the water, broken and bleeding and obviously getting their butt whipped, yet they don't seem to be trying to get out of the water. They remain engaged in crocodile wrestling. This is confusing because they look absolutely miserable, and you are worried about them. You try not to be rude, but you call out, "Hello there! Good day, mate! May I be so forward as to ask why in the world you don't get away from the crocodile?"

They look up from their bloody endeavor and respond, "I'm trying to figure out everything there is to know about crocodiles so I can keep myself safe from them! I need to see what their scales look like under their belly in order to know their breed. I need to know how old a particular crocodile is. I need to know how many teeth this crocodile is missing. I need to know all about crocodiles if I am going to stay safe from crocodiles! I can't possibly get out of the water!" Further confused, you might say, "Well, not to be rude mate, but it does not seem to be working, since that crocodile just bit off your toe."

Far too many of us are wrestling with crocodiles in our homes, trying to get them to change by understanding them better. Far too many of us question ourselves at work when a crocodile tries to bite us (or succeeds in doing so). Far too many of us are bloody and bruised from being raised by crocodiles, hoping they might turn into bunnies in their old age.

If we saw someone literally wrestling with a crocodile and not trying to get away, we would call them crazy, yet we fail to recognize the areas of our own lives in which we *are*, metaphorically speaking, wrestling crocodiles. We have crocodiles in our beds and in our heads. We see crocodiles in our work and in our worries. We find crocodiles in our families and in our feelings.

To stay safe from crocodiles, you don't have to learn how to be a better crocodile wrestler. You don't need to know every piece of information about the different types of crocodiles and why they bite. The strategies presented throughout this book are intended to keep you safe from crocodiles, not just clarify the differences within the species. Your toxic person may be the sociopath "breed" or the narcissist "breed" or the selfish jerk "breed." Here is the fact, Jack. All three breeds can gnaw your arm off. Many times, the safety we seek isn't found in a specific diagnosis; it's found in no longer putting yourself in a position to get bitten.

"But how do I know if I am just overreacting? How do I know if *I* am the toxic one? How do I know if there is really a problem or it was all in my head?" I can hear you asking any of all of these questions. (Hint: many of us secretly want to determine that the situation is our fault because, were that to be true, we could fix ourselves and remain in the relationship without having to move away from the crocodiles or identify which of us are crocs. More on this later!). If you are trying to figure out whether or not you have been wrestling a crocodile or wondering how to figure out who the crocodile is within a relationship, it is helpful to ask yourself the following questions:

- Was I in a relationship or situation where one person got to make the rules, enforce the rules, and break the rules? Was it my job to follow the rules?
- Did that person always get the better end of the deal, or did we truly take turns?
- Did they constantly play the victim and expect me to save them from their own bad decisions? Did they make me feel bad if I was unwilling to cover up their bad behavior?
- Did I get to a place where I trusted them more than I trusted myself? Did they become THE VOICE in my life?
- Did they encourage me to do what was good for me, or did they have a regular pattern of convincing me to do what was right for them?

- Did I ever leave conversations shell-shocked or confused about why I was unable to communicate my needs and come to a mutual win/win?
- Did I find myself taking responsibility for things that were not my responsibility (emotionally and/or in daily life) and doing all the work in the relationship? Were they telling me I needed to work even harder?
- Did I ever find myself on heightened alert around them? Did I feel like I was walking on eggshells? Did I notice myself changing my behavior to meet their expectations in situations where I should have been able to relax or be myself?
- Did I feel like it was impossible to stay on topic when I tried to bring up a concern? Did they flip everything around to avoid areas they needed to change?
- Did I notice them blaming me and others for their problems and consequences? Did they make everything everyone else's fault?

The more questions you answered yes to, the more toxic the behavior was. The more prevalent these patterns are in your relationship, the more likely it is that the relationship is a toxic one. No person or relationship is problem-free, but knowing whether or not you are in a truly toxic situation comes down to recognizing the *pattern* of those problems.

The more persistent the pattern, the more toxic the relationship.

We all have bad days, and none of us is perfect. Yet, if we *only* look at individual instances, we miss seeing the truth that lies before us. Be wary of looking at what happens in just one day as if those happenings are stand-alone incidents. Look for a *pattern* of anger, of image management, of responsibility avoidance, of control, or of blaming others.

There is a drastic difference between calling someone a bad name once during a disagreement and calling someone a bad name on a weekly basis for years. There is a drastic difference between not thinking that something is your fault and not thinking that *anything* is your fault. There is a drastic difference between losing your temper once and losing your temper weekly. There is a drastic difference between losing one job and not being able to hold down a job at all. There is a drastic difference between making one bad money decision and making regular bad money decisions.

There is a difference between a dog that bites you once and a dog that bites you daily.

To be clear, this may be the point where you start making excuses for the toxic person in your life and suggesting that his or her behavior is "not that bad." If you find yourself in this position, I need to tell you something. Please know that I am saying this with all the love, lollipops, and unicorn sprinkles I can muster. If you continue to make excuses for toxic behavior, you will never become Toxic Person Proof™. Please keep reading!

I know how difficult it can be to hold onto hope that someone will change. I struggled for *years* because I kept hoping crocodiles would turn into bunnies, if only I was patient enough. This life strategy did not lead me to success.

But other strategies *did* lead to success. And peace. And healthy relationships. And better days. And better weeks. And better years. Other strategies helped me learn to solve problems that had solutions rather than hope my problems would fix themselves. Other strategies helped me see the person rather than simply see the potential in that person. Other strategies helped me get to the real problem rather than try to figure out why toxic people kept telling me *I* was the problem.

These strategies are what I have outlined in these pages. May these strategies help you on your own journey of becoming Toxic Person Proof™.

PART 1

GETTING CONTROL OF YOUR HEAD, YOUR HEART AND YOUR LIFE

CHAPTER 1

PROTECTING THE ONE PERSON YOU ARE STUCK WITH FOR LIFE

"From the day you are born to the day you die, the only person you are really stuck with is yourself."

—Yours Truly

"Sarah, do you like taking personality quizzes?"

Um, do wolves like howling at the moon? Do superheroes dig tight tights and long capes? Do middle-aged women like a little shapewear between them and their jeans? Why yes, I do like personality tests!

Personality tests are fascinating to me because they never fail to teach me something about myself and others. I've taken thirty or more personality tests throughout the years, but the test I took on this particular day was even more revealing than normal. I sat and stared at the results multiple times:

"If there were a serial killer on the loose, your personality type would be the first to die among your friends. You would be in the shower singing show tunes and would never see your killer coming."

Dang it! I know some personality tests are more widely researched than others, and this particular quiz on "How Different Personalities Interact With Serial Killers" probably had little-to-no research attached to it, but I had conducted enough research throughout my own life to know the test results were accurate. My natural personality trait is "most likely to be killed. To be taken advantage of. To stumble into the arms of evil."

Truths about the old me:

1. At one point, I believed that pretty much everyone was good. Or that at least everyone I *knew* was good. I knew bad people existed, but they existed somewhere else. They weren't in my circle. They were on the news at 11:00 PM and in bars at 2:00 AM. They were in prisons and hung out in the parts of town my dad told me not to drive through. They were in the world, yes, but they weren't in *my* world.

2. I was quick to self-analyze. I believed I was responsible for my actions and reactions, I was quick to ask for forgiveness in hopes of moving on, and I wanted to "own my part" in conflict.

3. I sought out advice. I didn't think I was perfect, and I was looking for ways to constantly improve. When people had "wisdom" to give, I had ears willing to hear. When people told me that I needed to change something, I assumed they had my best interests at heart. I believed in my ability to change, as well as others' ability to change.

4. When people appeared confident, I believed they actually were confident. I assumed other people knew more than I did if they spoke with conviction. Obviously, there would be exceptions—people who talked just to hear themselves speak—but overall, I trusted what most people said.

5. I really, really liked people. I valued relationships over being right, making money, or getting credit for a completed project. I took pride in being a good friend. I was open and agreeable right from the start, which resulted in having a lot of friends.

6. I was really great at sticking up for other people. I actually spent a lifetime defending and befriending the underdog. I assumed everyone was looking to lift up others too. I happened to be much better at sticking up for others than I was at sticking up for myself.

7. I was a fabulous problem solver. I believed that if something wasn't working, you simply worked harder at it. When problems in my life popped up, I believed I could eventually figure them out. I just hadn't figured them out *yet*.

8. I wasn't a quitter. I was loyal and stuck through people's dark and difficult times. I didn't take the easy way, nor did I respect people who did.

9. I was strong enough to take it. If someone was having a bad day and took their anger or frustration out on me, I didn't let it bother me because I told myself they didn't have anyone else to get upset with. It was my "job" to be strong enough to take their mood, anger, hurt, or even trauma.

10. I was hopeful and optimistic. If life gives you lemons, you make lemonade. The sun will come out tomorrow. Things will get better if you just keep on keeping on. I always had the right meme, quote, verse, or affirmation to remind me to just keep doing me and let life handle the rest. Somebody else would take care of the hard stuff. I was not to worry my pretty little head over it.

11. I was independent. I loved my relationships but tried not to need much from others. I was more comfortable giving than taking. I thought this was what made me a good person.

12. I believed in giving to others. Putting others before myself. Being kind. Being selfless. Living by my values.

13. I had a heart bigger than my brain most of the time.

14. I assumed that if other people trusted someone, that person was safe to trust.

15. I made friends easily and was quick to have "real" conversations.

16. I thought that being honest meant being open.

17. I believed that it was important to see the best in people.

18. I believed in second chances. And third chances. And 150th chances.
19. I believed that forgiving someone meant I had to let them back into my life as if nothing happened.
20. I believed in time. I believed that if you waited around and did the right thing, God, the Universe, a boss, or maybe a fairy godmother would swoop in and hand me a gold star and say, "You did it! You put up with hard things for long enough! Congratulations. You passed the test. Here is your gold star, and now the person/situation is going to change completely, and it will all work out. You just earned your happily ever after! Well done. Good thing you hung in there!"

While I have certainly made significant gains in these aspects of my personality (which is a good thing since you are reading my book on becoming Toxic Person Proof™), I have certainly been hurt by toxic people. I knew I had to change because my life experience when I was not being Toxic Person Proof™ was so painful that I didn't think I could live through another round of toxic person encounters. My mom and dad call it learning the hard way. I'd been hurt too many times not to make change. My kindness had been used against me. I kept giving out olive branches and getting smacked in the face by them. I kept thinking that people would be different the next time. I kept thinking that people actually wanted to change. I kept thinking that if I did the right thing, others would do the right thing.

I believed that people were basically good, usually helpful, and mostly honest. I thought they wanted the best for others. I thought they wanted the best for me. (And, for the most part, I still believe that many humans still want the best for me.)

But, I don't believe that *all* humans want the best for me. Nor do I believe that *all* humans are safe for me. I now believe that it is my responsibility to keep myself safe and work to know the difference between people who are safe for me and those who aren't.

I know it seems highly evolved to say, "Everyone has the potential to be better. All we need is love! All we need is time! All we need is better communication!" Positive psychology sells for a reason. We WANT it to be true. We don't want the people in our life to have personality traits that aren't likely to change. We want to believe they can change. We tell ourselves that they MUST change. That they aren't doing it on purpose. That if they knew better, they would do better. Optimism is hopeful, and yet for those of us having toxic person encounters, optimism is a trap.

Because of our positive and hopeful beliefs regarding humanity, most of us have spent more time researching the perfect morning coffee than we have researching how to keep ourselves safe from people who could hurt us. We think that if we don't want something to be true and we don't think about it being true, then it won't be true. Psychologists call it denial. Our friends call it stupidity. I call it having your hope and kindness used against you. If you would not hurt someone on purpose, it is easy to believe they would not hurt you on purpose. If they aren't hurting you on purpose, then their mistreatment of you was an accident, and you can keep believing the best about them. If it was just an accident, it is easy to believe them when they tell you it won't happen again. Hope can be a difficult thing to let go of—even if someone has done the exact same thing twenty times previously. Your hope will lie to you and tell you that time number twenty-one will be different. You can see, I hope (pun intended), why being hopeful is not always helpful. This way of thinking leads to a pattern of looking past repeated bad behaviors and bad days. It leads to a pattern of seeing the potential in people rather than the patterns in people. Actions *should* speak louder than words.

Only after opening your eyes do you start learning how to find the right kind of people to get into business with. The right kind of people to get into bed with. The right kind of people to have around your children. The right kind of people to help you care for an aging parent. The right kind of people to tell you who God is. The right kind of people to tell you who *you* are.

WHY WE DON'T SPOT TOXIC PEOPLE

Our brains often find creative ways to save energy that isn't always in our best interest. For example, our brains tell us that we are "safer" on our couch than we are exercising.
Couch? Easy! Safe! Comfort zone!
Exercise? Vulnerable! Effort! Sweat!

Our brains try to prevent extra work by talking us out of exercise. But there is a reason we say, "Pay now and play later." The work of exercise today can prevent the work of disease later. Healthy eating today can prevent the work of extra weight later. Investing in ourselves today can prevent the work of emotional, financial, or even spiritual problems later. Yet, our brains like to take the easy way out and tell us two lies:

1. We don't have to worry about that because it won't happen to us. (Denial)
2. If we do have to worry about it, it is better to push off the worry to tomorrow instead of thinking about it today. (Delay)

People who tell themselves they don't have to worry about becoming Toxic Person Proof™ maintain the same line of thinking as do people who say they don't have to get off the couch. Or diet. Or save for retirement. Or quit smoking. Or go to the doctor. Or whatever safety component your own brain likes to push off. If you have been belittled for having a toxic person encounter, I hope this helps you forgive yourself. People want to tell themselves they won't have a toxic person encounter as long as they do everything "right." They blame you in order to feel safe. In most cases, they have missed identifying toxic people in their own lives, too, but blaming you or making you feel dumb or small helps them separate themselves from the reality that they could be conned or manipulated as well.

You can't become Toxic Person Proof™ if you tell yourself there are no toxic people out there. As Sandra L. Brown, founder of

The Institute for Relational Harm Reduction & Public Pathology Education, said, "You can't solve what you can't see."[1]

It is easier to believe everyone is good for us and we don't have to sharpen our skills to protect ourselves against toxic person encounters. It is easier to believe that all the toxic people are in jail or someone else's neighborhood. Yet, we know this can't possibly be true. You can imagine the stories I hear when I say I'm a toxic relationship specialist. People say, "Well, I've got a story for you! I've got this niece, this mom, this coworker, this uncle, this friend, this girl, this guy..."

Most people believe that toxic people exist. Most people don't believe they are being fooled by toxic people. They think toxic people encounters only happen to everyone else.

HIDING: THE OTHER SIDE OF THE HOUSE

Before you slip into "Everyone is horrible and I will just hide in my house!" know that this is just your brain trying to keep you safe rather than make you happy.

There is a difference between someone who is still breathing and someone who is truly alive. I have seen people trust no one in an effort to stay safe. I've seen people give up on love. Give up on friendship. Give up on fun. Give up on connection. They think they are playing it safe, but the statistics around loneliness are clear. Having healthy relationships is good for us. Loneliness is *not* good for us. You can enjoy being alone. That's great! I wrote this book alone. I meditate alone. I practice piano alone. I usually do yoga alone.

But I have the choice not to be alone. To pick up the phone and giggle with a friend. To wrap my arms around my husband as he sleeps. To collaborate with other experts. To phone a friend if the questions get too tough on a game show. Freedom is the feeling of having the choice. Think about the difference between taking a week-long vacation from work and being furloughed. In both scenarios, you get time off, but in only one scenario do you have the choice to work or not work. Being Toxic Person Proof™ isn't about hiding. It's about having choices. It's about learning to be confident in your ability to move forward in relationships and protect yourself as you move forward.

THE MESSY MIDDLE

The purpose of this work is to find the middle. To find out how to be least likely to get killed by a serial killer and most likely to have a life full of love, laughter, and camaraderie. A life in which you know who to get in bed with and who to go into business with. A life of being Toxic Person Proof™.

WHY WE DON'T PROTECT OURSELVES

Growing up, most of us were not taught balance as we learned to protect ourselves. Some of us may have been taught people are crazy and that the only people you could trust were the members of your family (which worked pretty well until you realized some members of your family were also crazy!). Some of us learned through words and experience to expect others to disappoint us, because people are disappointing. Others of us were raised to take care of everyone else. "Love others as yourself" may well have been translated as loving everyone *except* yourself. We learned that our purpose was to help others, give to others, listen to others, and please others.

I remember going to buy bread with my grandmother and son one day. They began talking about a kid at school who was bullying other children. My grandmother said, "Well if he's being mean to people, he probably just needs a friend. You should make more of an effort to be friends with him."

"Ahhhh!" I thought. "That is where it all starts." **The belief that if someone is acting badly toward you, you should change your behavior so they will change their behavior.** The belief that if someone else is making bad choices, then it's your job to change yourself to help them. The belief that there must be a

10

good reason for them to be mean to you, and if you give more of yourself away to them, they will be nice to you. The belief that if someone is hurting you, you should give them more access to you. The belief that you should be willing to do the emotional work of the relationship.

My grandmother wasn't trying to put my son or me in a position to be hurt, of course. She, like so many of us, simply believed that if you were nice to people, they would be nice back. She saw things from her own perspective. She believed that the reason difficult people harm others is because they are hurting. Consequently, the way to keep them from hurting people is to give them more love. More attention. More access. More of you.

My grandmother is far from the only person who reinforces this belief. Helpers, healers, pastors, therapists, social workers, advocates, good girls, nice guys, people who care, people who believe in humankind, people who believe the best in others, and people who believe in change reinforce it as well.

I remember the story of Laura, a young teenager who was having trouble with a friend at school. The friend had been spreading mean messages and turning other people against Laura out of jealousy, and despite Laura's many attempts, she could not get the girl to stop being mean. Her school counselor said Laura should start buying the girl coffee in the mornings in an effort to improve the friendship. When Laura asked what I thought she should do, I suggested she use her money to buy coffee for the friend who was already good to her.

Teaching kids and teens lessons such as "The worse you are to me, the nicer I will be to you" sets young people up for a lifetime of trouble! In another school setting, I heard of a teacher putting the nicest girl in the class beside the biggest troublemaker. The little girl's mother told me that the boy kept kicking her under the desk, but the young girl didn't let it bother her! While I have great grace for overworked and underpaid teachers, I did not agree with the teacher's decision! Kids don't need to be taught to get better at handling disrespectful and even violent people. Nor do they need to learn that it is their job to put up with disrespectful or violent behavior to help out the teacher and other classmates. The lessons we learn as kids shape our futures, and I want to see futures with more people aware of how to protect themselves from toxic behavior.

HOW TO PROTECT YOURSELF

One of the best ways to protect yourself is to move toward people who are kind to you and away from people who are mean to you. Believe people's actions rather than just focusing on their words. If someone kicks you, it is okay to ask for a different seat. If there is a bully in school, do your best to stay away from him or her. If there is a girl who continually spreads rumors about you, don't take her a coffee! Save your money and your kindness for the friend who is willing to stand up for you when things are hard!

In its simplest form, the lesson is this: The quickest way to protect yourself against toxic people is by giving toxic people less access to you. Not by having better boundaries. Not by standing up for yourself. Not by being better at handling conflict. Not by healing the wounds of your inner child! The best way to protect yourself from toxic people is to learn to recognize toxicity and stay away from toxicity. The next quickest way to protect yourself is to learn how to stop allowing others to use your kindness against you. To learn who is safe to give your kindness to and who to avoid.

Perhaps a story will illustrate this point. Once upon a time a young girl was walking along a mountain path to her grandmother's house when she heard a rustle at her feet. Looking down, she saw a snake, but before she could react, the snake spoke to her.

"I am about to die," he said. "It's too cold for me up here, and I am freezing. There is no food in these mountains, and I am starving. Please, put me under your coat and take me with you."

"No," the girl replied. "I know your kind. You are a rattlesnake. And if I pick you up, you will bite me, and your bite is poisonous."

"No, no," the snake said. "If you help me, you will be my best friend. I will treat *you* differently."

The young girl sat down on a rock for a moment to rest and think things over. She looked at the beautiful markings on the snake and had to admit he *was* the most beautiful snake she had ever seen.

Suddenly, she said, "I believe you. I will save you. *All living things deserve to be treated with kindness.*"

She then reached over, put the snake gently under her coat, and continued toward her grandmother's house.

Within a moment, she felt a sharp pain in her side. The snake had bitten her!

"How could you do this to me?" she cried. "You promised that you would not bite me, and I trusted you!"

"You knew what I was when you picked me up," he hissed as he slithered away.

Why did the snake bite? Was it because she held him wrong? No! Was it because she wasn't nice enough? No! Was it because she said the wrong thing? No! The snake bit her because the snake was close to her. The girl didn't need to learn how to handle snakes better. The girl needed to learn to stay away from snakes. Stop pretending that snakes are not snakes. Stop making excuses for snakes because they are pretty. Stop trying to be so nice that the snake will be nice back. "You knew who I was when you picked me up."

When people show you who they are, believe them.

WHAT ASPECTS OF YOUR CHARACTER MAKE YOU VULNERABLE?

We all have aspects of our personalities that make us vulnerable. It might be a need for loyalty, a fear of change, a desire to avoid admitting you made the wrong choice, a reluctance to start over, hoping to be seen as a good parent, or wanting to be seen as having a strong faith practice. We ALL have desires that other people could manipulate if they wanted to. If it isn't your kindness, maybe it is your desire to succeed. Or your belief that things will get better with time. Or your desire to keep your family together. We all have strings that people can pull to make us jump and get us to do what they want. To become Toxic Person Proof™ and protect ourselves, we had better know ourselves well enough to know where we are vulnerable.

"To guard against victimization, you must: be free of potentially harmful misconceptions about human nature and behavior; know how to correctly assess the character of others; have high self-awareness, **especially regarding those aspects of your own character that might increase your vulnerability to manipulation**; recognize and correctly label the tactics of manipulation and respond to them appropriately; and avoid fighting losing battles." - George K. Simon Jr., *In Sheep's Clothing: Understanding and Dealing with Manipulative People*

Before we figure out what makes you vulnerable, I want to point out that your strengths can absolutely be used against you. This is not a conversation about what is wrong with you. This is a conversation about what personality traits, ideals, and values you hold that someone could pull on if they wanted to get you to dance like a puppet. If you want to become Toxic Person Proof™ and figure out how to protect yourself, we need to think much more broadly than "had a bad childhood, has daddy issues, or parents got divorced." Those are things that have happened to you, not your personality traits. Let's look at an example of the difference.

"One of the most common character traits I have witnessed among survivors is their ability and desire to be **self-reflective.** As a generalization, most survivors are able to **critically look at their own behaviors and motives**. They are **willing to fix character** defects within themselves. These personal strengths are precisely what narcissists, sociopaths, and psychopaths exploit. A toxic person knows if they hurl accusations at a survivor, those words will pierce deep and cause the survivor to look **inwards to see if the accusations are true**. It is the toxic person who needs to do more self-reflection but that will never, never happen." - Shannon Thomas, *Healing from Hidden Abuse*

We think of self-reflection and the ability to look inside ourselves in order to improve as good qualities. However, as Thomas points out, those traits can also be a good thing for narcissists, sociopaths, and psychopaths. Self-reflection is a great example of a positive personality trait that can be used against you.

Sandra L. Brown points this out in her book, *Women Who Love Psychopaths*, as well. During her thirty-three years of studying psychopathy and their victims, she came up with the theme of super traits. She noticed how many people who had toxic person encounters were both conscientious and agreeable. She describes these super traits as "doing the right thing, a life guided by goals, beliefs, values, and the steady application of all necessary resources to meet those goals." On page 259, Brown also says that people who have had toxic person encounters "follow conventional forms of integrity -not lying, cheating, stealing, no violence, responsible to authority and not bucking the system - **a high degree of integrity.**" Brown goes on to say, "This is the deep ingrained truth of their personality. They have clear levels of right and wrong and they live out their principles."

I believe this is why people of strong character and values fail to identify the signs in toxic people. They have such strong personal integrity that they expect others to have personal integrity as well! Toxic people know how to use what is good about you for their own good. They know that if you have a strong work ethic, they can get you to work harder. They know that if you don't want to fail, you will put up with a lot of bad behavior rather than end the relationship with the toxic person. They know that if you are not a quitter, you won't give up—even when the toxic person encounter is killing you.

A desire to be needed is one of the most popular personality traits toxic people exploit. This trait is both a strength and a weakness. People who want to be needed say things like, "I just want to help" or "I come alive when I take care of others" or "I just feel bad." Unfortunately, I have never seen the need to be needed get people the life and love they desired, but I *have* seen it wear a lot of really great people down!

Wanting to help others is a fabulous trait. The world is better when it is full of people who help others. But don't allow this trait to leave you vulnerable. There are two types of people in the world: those looking to get help and those looking to help themselves. In his book *Character Disturbances*, George Simon told the joke of two social workers being robbed. Instead of calling the police to get their wallets back, they ran after the robber and yelled, "Stop! We can help you get your life back in order. Let us help you!" The robber took something from them, but instead of protecting themselves, the social workers' first thought was, "How can we help the robber change?" While helping others is a wonderful personality trait, it should not be at the cost of our own safety. Chasing someone who just robbed you and trying to talk them into changing is a bad idea. Trying to get toxic people to change is almost always a bad idea as well.

It is often the things that have made us successful in other areas of life that leave us vulnerable to toxic people. We will explore this in depth in the chapter on "smart-girl/guy syndrome." For now, take a minute and reflect on what aspects of your personality could leave you vulnerable.

Questions to figure out what makes you vulnerable:

1. Is there a personality trait or value people can use to convince you to change your mind?
2. What value or personality trait do you most want to defend? What do you hold most dear?
3. If you set a boundary and someone wanted to get you to drop your boundary, what value or personality trait would they bring up?
4. What value or personality trait would someone need to bring up if they wanted to make you start questioning yourself and your decisions?
5. What type of conversation or event gets the strongest reaction out of you?
6. Do you notice a pattern when it comes to the ways people get you to change your mind about things?
7. What value or personality trait has been used against you in the past?

8. What value or personality trait most shapes how you view the world and others?

Summary: You have to learn about yourself in order to protect yourself. Simply studying traits exhibited by toxic people or understanding personality disorders is not enough. Figure out what values, strengths, or beliefs make you vulnerable to toxic people. If you are unaware of your vulnerabilities toxic people will use your best traits against you.

CHAPTER 2
LEARNING TO SEE RED FLAGS

When people tell you who they are, believe them.
—Maya Angelou

Before I met my husband, I scoured the internet for "Red Flags To Look For In Dating". The lists I came across were humorous at best and concerning at worst. The internet—in all its infinite wisdom—told me to watch out for guys with big arm muscles because they were probably narcissists. Thankfully, I didn't listen to that one; my husband looks amazing in a tank top.

Other red flag lists were super generic and general. They included items such as "watch out for controlling behavior," "watch out for someone who lies," "watch out for someone who flirts with people at work," "watch out for someone who mistreats his mother," and "watch out for someone who thinks pineapple doesn't belong on pizza."

Truthfully, I added the last one. Hawaiian pizza is my fave.

I can't tell you how many times I've gotten on the phone with someone who begins the conversation by asking me for a list of red flags. I'm sure they do so because they hope having a simple checklist will be enough to make them Toxic Person Proof™. However, only knowing what to watch out for doesn't seem to be enough protect us from a toxic person encounter. We have to know what we are going to do with the knowledge. I would bet you an extra- large pizza that if I lined up a group of thirteen-year-old girls and went through a list of red flags with them, they would know which issues should warrant concern.

"Raise your hand if you want a friend who lies. No takers? Got it. Okay then, raise your hand if you want to work for a controlling boss. Who wants a boyfriend with a string of ex-girlfriends who hate his guts and refer to him as a narcissist? No one? Okay, who hopes their future spouse likes to flirt with other people? Anyone looking for a roommate who can't seem to hold onto a job?" Thirteen-year-old girls would easily recognize these issues as problematic! But would anyone be willing to bet that if this same group of girls answered these questions immediately after turning thirteen, they'd go on to be Toxic Person Proof™ at thirty-three? I certainly would not! Just because these girls could recognize red flags once upon a time does not mean they are going to know how to protect themselves against relationships with red flags down the road. There is often a disconnect between what we know and what we do.

People don't need a PhD in psychology to recognize red flags, yet great people keep having toxic person encounters. Companies hire people based on charisma while ignoring holes in their resume. Men and women keep thinking that if only they become successful enough, they can finally, *finally* make a toxic parent happy. Successful men fall for female leeches who are looking to avoid any and all responsibility in their lives and draw people in with their sob stories. Smart women can't seem to accept how predictably unpredictable their boyfriend is, so they ignore the warnings of their friends.

The problem isn't that we don't know what the red flags are. The problem is that we don't want the red flags to exist, so we pretend they don't.

We talk ourselves out of the red flags we see. Our brains are tricky suckers, and they try to conserve energy. That's why it is easier to sit down than stand up. It's easier to fall into worry than practice problem solving. It's the same reason why many of us avoid change like the plague, and avoid taking action like it's a night without Netflix. It's the reason why it's easier to eat Nutella straight out of the jar than to chop and roast carrots. Our brain likes to keep things easy. It likes to compartmentalize.

Our brains work against us in five main ways:

1. Our brains like to tell us that if there really were a problem, we would see it.
2. Our brains tell us that if we can convince ourselves there is no problem then the problem won't exist.
3. Our brains hide the things we don't want to see.
4. Our brains tell us we can fix the problem with enough work.
5. Our brains tell us that we ourselves are the problem. It is easier to change ourselves than it is to change someone else, so if we can convince ourselves that we are the problem, we can also convince ourselves that we are the solution.

Toxic people know how our brains work and they love this. Love it. As in, *looooooove* it. It ensures that we do the work of the relationship while they reap the rewards. It is also a way that toxic people dangle hope in front of others. The recipient keeps hoping things will get better, if he or she can figure out what needs to change about themselves. The toxic person ends up not having to change anything.

A list of red flags is not enough. Researching toxic personalities is not enough. In order to become Toxic Person Proof™, you have to accept the following truths and stop talking yourself out of them:

1. There are toxic people in this world, and you know them.
2. Toxic people know what they are doing.
3. The more emotionally connected you are to the hope that someone is not toxic, the more likely you will be to overlook toxic behavior.
4. When you want to believe something, your brain will trick you into seeing what you want to see and believing what you want to believe. I'll cover this further in chapter 4.

5. The safest way to keep away from toxic people is to be on the lookout for them.

Let's break it down, shall we?

THERE ARE TOXIC PEOPLE

"I just can't believe anyone would ever do that on purpose."
—Amy

"It's hard for me to believe there are people who act like this."
—Mike

Crucial truth: everyone isn't like you. This understanding is as crucial to a successful human experience as is learning that it isn't appropriate for you to suck on your toes after your first birthday.

It is unlikely that in this day and age you believe everyone likes the same music you do. You've probably come to realize that not everyone likes your favorite TV shows. You understand that some people are more outgoing than you are, while some are less outgoing than you are. You understand that some prefer eating with their right hand, while others prefer using their left hand.

After you think about the amazing combinations that make you you, and make me me, and make your great uncle Fred smelly and hairy, you can probably agree that not everyone is like you. At this point, you are probably saying, "Wow, Sarah, thanks for that eternal truth. Life changing." Yeah, I get it. It seems simple. Yet we forget it. All the time.

When it comes to dealing with others, we see things from our own perspectives. If we treat people with dignity and respect, we assume others will treat us with dignity and respect. If we strive to be our best, we assume others want to do and be their best. If we don't try to gain the upper hand over others in conversations, we assume others aren't trying to gain the upper hand over us. If we don't regularly manipulate and lie to get our way, we are less likely to look for others who manipulate and lie to get their way. If we wouldn't destroy someone else's reputation just because we didn't get our way, we aren't likely to assume anyone else would. If we don't think we deserve to always win, we aren't as likely to realize that someone else is always getting the better end of the deal in the relationship. If we are willing to take turns, we are not as likely to catch on that it is always someone else's turn. If we wouldn't cheat on the business that supports us or cheat on the man who loves us, we assume others aren't happily having their cake and eating it too.

Everyone isn't like you, nor is everyone like me. The more likely we are to see the best in people, the less likely we are to see the worst in people. Becoming Toxic Person Proof™ is about finding a balance. Assuming everyone is like us causes us to miss the true data before us. These assumptions cause us to miss the opportunity to identify toxic people. We assume the best, that they didn't mean whatever they did, that a behavior isn't reflective of who they really are, or that we are wrong. "The flag isn't really red," we tell ourselves. "We are just being too judgy/picky/mean."

Think about how often you say things like:

"I can't believe he would do that."

"Who acts like that?"

"What kind of person doesn't…"

"You would think someone of her age would know better."

"You think they would know how to act by now."

"I can't believe she said that."

We unconsciously utter phrases like this because we believe others think the same way we do. We believe our perspective is the standard for human behavior. When others don't act in the same way we would, we put their behavior in the category of "unbelievable." If you want to become Toxic Person Proof™, you have to start by believing and accepting that there are people whose values, thought processes, brain structures, experiences, and desires are different from yours.

"But Sarah, we all have bad days and things that are not perfect. Don't hurt people hurt people? Shouldn't we all get a little grace?"

Yes, of course. We do all need and deserve a little grace from time to time, but we also need to be wiser about who we give that grace to. Many of us also need to be wiser about how long we give grace.

The problem comes when our thought processes end up helping the toxic people rather than helping ourselves. When we get out of balance and give *all* grace, we miss the truth. We don't miss these red flags because we are stupid; we just assume the other person must have a really, really good reason to behave badly! If we would never be toxic on purpose, they must not be doing it on purpose either! We see from our own perspective and miss what they are doing.

Unfortunately, our attention shifts to the reason behind their bad behavior rather than focusing on their bad behavior. When we are trying to figure why they are acting badly then we forget to take action to ensure the bad behavior doesn't hurt us again. When we see a red flag, we try to figure out why the flag is red rather than realize the red flag is a signal of danger. We see a red flag and assume their childhood is the problem or their past is the problem. We lose sight of the fact that their *behavior* is the problem. Toxic people know that if they can send you into overthinking and have you trying to figure out why the flag is red, you will offer sympathy and empathy rather than demand their accountability.

THERE ARE TOXIC PEOPLE IN THIS WORLD, AND YOU KNOW THEM

Have you ever watched a show on criminal behavior where they interviewed a neighbor who exclaimed, "I can't believe this! She seemed like such a nice lady; I had no idea."

Have you ever watched a business fall apart because someone brought in a friend of a friend? Perhaps you thought, "Well, my friend trusted him, so I thought I could trust him."

Have you ever told someone something horrible that someone else had done and heard them respond, "They would never do that! I know them."

Life would be a lot easier for us if toxic people carried pitch forks, had pointy black beards, and sported tails, but they don't. Accept this and believe it. If you don't believe toxic people exist, you will always be vulnerable to them. Toxic people are great at making sure you see the version of them that they want you to see.

"She's the last person you would suspect."

"I had no idea."

"She seemed so helpful."

"He seemed so charming."

"She seemed so happy."

"I never imagined someone in that type of position would behave that badly."

At one point, Bill Cosby was one of the most loved men in America. When the sexual assault charges started to pour in, we tried to balance images of a comedian performing living room dance routines with accounts of rape. We smiled as Cosby told us jokes and sold us pudding, and then cringed as woman after woman came forward and told the same story. At one point, most of us believed Cosby was an example of all that was right with humanity. We were tricked. Others knew an entirely different version of Cosby, when the lights were off and the door was locked.

Bill Cosby was once the neighbor of Jeffrey Epstein. Epstein is another great example of someone who presented himself one way in public and behaved another way in private. His name is now synonymous with sex trafficking minors, among other scandals. However, his name used to be connected with success and power, with close associations with multiple presidents, Stephen Hawking, and Prince Andrew of the British royal family.[1] At one point, Berni Madoff was a person people were happy to listen to (and give their money to). Earlier in my life, it would have been ridiculous to imagine young boys being taken advantage of by priests.

Remember when we thought Monica Lewinsky was lying? Remember when companies clamored to have OJ Simpson's beautiful smile promote their product? Remember when Mel Gibson was championed by Christians as a hero when he created "The Passion of The Christ?" This movie was released a few years before

Gibson allegedly broke the teeth of his ex-girlfriend while she was holding their eight-month-old child. When asked to apologize, he is quoted as having said, "She deserved it."[2]

Eight out of ten teenage and child rape victims know their perpetrator. When authorities talk to victims of sexual violence, it comes to light that the perpetrator is nearly always someone they know. The uncle. The teacher. The older cousin. The guy from chemistry class. Dr. Martha Stout, long time Harvard psychologist and author of *The Sociopath Next Door* estimates that one in every twenty-five people is a sociopath.[3] The American Academy of Physicians has stated that 14.9% of Americans age eighteen and over qualify as having at least one personality disorder.[4] The National Institute of Mental Health estimates that 9.1% of Americans has a personality disorder.[5] In an interview I had with Sandra L. Brown, CEO of The National Institute for Relational Harm Reduction, she estimated that one in five Americans has some type of personality disorder.[6] Statistically, you are going to be around people with personality disorders, and people with personality disorders exhibit toxic behavior.

I am aware that the statistics put out by different groups are not all exactly the same, mainly because toxic people rarely ever get help because they don't think they have a problem. However, the statistics do agree that there are toxic people out there, and you know them.

History is filled with stories of people we admired for a time, people we later found out were lying to us. Toxic behavior leaves a trail. Throughout human history, there have been red flags that people saw—and then ignored. There were red flags that people talked about and then talked themselves out of because they didn't want to see the warnings. Lists of red flags will never be truly helpful if we cannot accept that there are toxic people out there, we are going to come across them during our lifetime, and they are not wearing a devil costume. Furthermore, lists of red flags will never be truly helpful if we continue to talk ourselves out of the red flags we do see.

The data is clear: none of us is exempt from toxic person encounters. None of us will completely avoid interacting with someone who is not operating by normal social standards of positive and decent behavior. Even the most conservative statistics agree that if we know and interact with more than twenty-five people, we know at least one toxic person. There is at least one person in your life who wouldn't think twice about ruining your life or the lives of others. There is at least one person who turns on the charm or the pity party in public, and then takes the mask off in private.

That confirms that both you and I know toxic people.

WHY IS THIS SO HARD TO BELIEVE?

Telling ourselves that everyone is good (or that nearly everyone we know is good) has helped us as a society in many ways throughout history. We are social creatures. Our default position is us versus them. For years, this mentality kept us alive in our tribal communities. We told ourselves that the people familiar to us were safe, while people from other tribal communities were not.

As children, we grew up hearing "Don't talk to strangers" rather than "Don't talk to sociopaths." Somehow, our parents thought the sociopaths were always people outside our circle of supposed safety. We think the sociopaths are people we haven't met. Despite the data, which says these personalities are on the rise rather than the decline, we tell ourselves that we are special. God, life, the Universe, however you choose to look at it, has somehow made our circle of influence different. We tell ourselves that our neighborhoods, our religious communities, our country clubs, and our workplaces are safe. Those other neighborhoods, those other religious communities, and those other work settings are where the bad people are.

History teaches us that toxic people are good at tricking people, and sometimes it is easier to let them trick us than to call out their bad behavior. Remember when I said sections of this book may make you mad? This might be one of those times! I understand why you might not want to believe that you know toxic people. I lived it, and I have talked to countless others about this. Your brain wants you to believe that you don't have to worry about this. That you've got this. Remember, your brain wants to save energy, and it doesn't want to be bothered with having to filter through people's personalities in order to stay safe. There is football to watch and dishes to be done! Your brain therefore decides "Ain't nobody got time for that!"

When we break down our thoughts in this way and compare them to the data regarding how many toxic people live among us, we can more easily see how ridiculous (and dangerous) our thinking is. Unfortunately, however, we usually operate from our default approach. That default approach is more helpful to toxic people than it is to us because it ignores the fact that at least one out of every ten people you know has traits of a toxic personality. Statistically, we all know and interact with toxic people on a regular basis. Did you hear that? All of us. That means you too. Stop that voice in your head that is trying to excuse yourself as the exception to the rule. I've played that game before. It's a ridiculous game with horrible results for you, as it makes you more susceptible to toxic people's manipulation.

ARE THEY REALLY EVERYWHERE?

"We serial killers are your sons, your husbands. We are everywhere."

—Ted Bundy

Ted Bundy and other serial killers are way outside of the scope of the toxic people most of us deal with on a regular basis, but toxic people don't have to be serial killers to harm us physically, psychologically, emotionally, socially, or financially. The point Bundy makes is that there are toxic people out there, and you know them.

Toxic people are also really good at operating among us. There is no toxic person watchlist for non-violent and non-criminal behavior. This is what makes this process difficult and why it is so important to become Toxic Person Proof™. For example, Shawn meets Kara on an online dating app. He seems nice and makes a great first impression. Kara can't look up a news story or criminal record to see that he has fathered four children with three different women, has cheated on every one of those women, and calls all three of them crazy for being upset by his bad behavior. He does tell Kara about the one time his wife threw him out of the house for being a little late. Kara agrees that the ex was overreacting and begins to feel sorry for Shawn. The game has begun. If you asked thirteen-year-old Kara if it was a red flag to have four children by three different women and a history of infidelity, she would likely say that it was. But Shawn is a master manipulator, and Kara is really tired of the dating scene. She recognizes and empathizes with Shawn's difficult childhood, and before the waiter brings the check during their first date, she starts to wonder who Shawn could be if only he understood what it was like to be well-loved.

It's tempting to comfort ourselves with the belief that only people in the dating pool need to worry about becoming Toxic Person Proof™, but the same people manipulating their dates are also manipulating their coworkers. Samantha isn't a serial killer, and she has no police record. What the hiring director doesn't know is that Samantha swindled money from her last job and blackmailed her boss to avoid having that fact show up on her work history. Samantha's resume is perfect, and her interview answers are flawless. Plus, the hiring director desperately needs to fill the spot, or her boss is going to be mad. So, Samantha gets hired and the business opens its doors to a toxic person encounter. Kara and the hiring director both missed the fact that there are toxic people everywhere, and they therefore need to proceed with caution when hiring new employees. If stories don't line up or facts seem to be missing, these are red flags worth paying attention to.

Summary: There are toxic people out there, and you know them. Your brain talks you out of seeing them so that your brain can conserve energy. Being Toxic Person Proof™ allows you to recognize when your brain falls into the pattern so you can protect yourself against faulty thinking. Many intelligent people throughout history have missed the early signs exhibited by toxic people! Having had a toxic person encounter doesn't make you stupid, but moving forward, you need to learn new skills in order to best protect yourself.

Of the areas covered so far, which is the biggest struggle for you? Do you tell yourself there aren't really toxic people out there in the world? Do you tell yourself that you are the exception to the rule and that the people around you are all safe? Do you tell yourself that certain people don't mean to act the way they act? Do you tell yourself that, with a little help from you, certain people will want to behave better? Give yourself the gift of ten minutes to really reflect on what areas you need to strengthen in order to become Toxic Person Proof™.

CHAPTER 3
YES, TOXIC PEOPLE KNOW
WHAT THEY ARE DOING

"I have concluded the main reason these predators are so successful in manipulating others. It lies not so much in their highly effective knowledge and use of manipulation tactics, but **rather in the reluctance of normal individuals to make harsh judgements about others**. Or to trust their gut instincts about the kind of person they are probably dealing with. They don't attach enough significance to the gift of fear and mistrust their instincts. On top of it all they are also often blinded by the notion promoted by traditional psychologies over the years that everyone is basically good and most especially just like them underneath their wall of defenses. So they allow themselves to believe that a person will only behave badly when hurting, frightened or in some type of inner pain. Such beliefs allow them to be easily victimized by the truly heartless."
—George K Simon, Character Disturbance

"Okay, Sarah, so I can accept that there are toxic people out there and that I know them, but they aren't actually doing it on purpose, right? Hurt people just need love. They just need help. They just need mentoring or a little patience. They just need therapy. They don't mean to be mean."

30

Once we really, truly accept that there are toxic people out there and that we know them, the next most important piece in becoming Toxic Person Proof™ is understanding that these people know exactly what they are doing. Toxic people know they are manipulating our kindness, avoiding responsibility, flipping everything to make it our fault, and playing the victim when it helps them get their way.

The study of personality disorders can feel like an endless tunnel of information. Is it nature? Is it nurture? Can they change? We do have one answer, and it is a prevalent one coming from people specializing in personality disorders, manipulation, con-artists, cult leaders, and swindlers: Yes, they know what they are doing.

That teenager telling you that his failures are because of your parenting style? Yep, he knows what he is doing. That "friend" at work who is always talking you into helping her out? Yes, she knows what she is doing. The husband who loses his temper at home but never in front of the people he wants to impress? Yes, him too. That sister who always knows just how to make you feel bad? Yep, her too.

In his bestselling book, *Why Does He Do That? Inside The Minds Of Angry And Controlling Men*, author and abuse expert Lundy Bancroft says that it is as though they went to school to learn how to do this. When you study manipulation and power dynamics, you will be shocked by how similar toxic people's strategies are. They are masters at their craft. They are masters at getting their way, avoiding accountability, minimizing their faults, and maximizing *your* faults. They get away with this behavior because we aren't looking for it, and when we *do* see it, we tend to make excuses for it. We assume they don't know what they are doing because the idea that they know what they are doing is nearly incomprehensible. Remember, everyone doesn't think the same way you do.

Far too often, we don't focus on a toxic person's behavior at all. We take our eyes off the *what* and focus our attention on the *why*.

What: What behavior are they displaying?

Why: Why are they acting that way?

If someone is acting out of character, figure out why. If someone is exhibiting a continued pattern of toxic behavior, however, don't be manipulated or taken with the why. Address the behavior rather than getting sucked into figuring out the reason behind it. Talk about what behavior they are regularly displaying rather than psychoanalyzing why they are doing it. Ask them to change their behavior if they want to be close to you. I know it seems counterintuitive to stop figuring them out, but remember, our goal is to start believing people when they tell us who they are. We need to stop seeing a pattern of behavior and telling ourselves, "Well, this isn't who they really are. If I can just figure out why they act that way, they will change their behavior and be a different person." No…no they won't.

Let's discuss the real *why* behind toxic people's behavior.

THEY SEE NO REASON TO CHANGE WHAT THEY ARE DOING

Toxic people hurt others. They don't play by the same set of rules, they don't take responsibility, and their lives show a pattern of problems—if you look for the pattern. This is an issue for the people who interact with toxic people, but it's not an issue for the toxic people themselves.

Let's imagine that you have found a magic pill that allows you not to feel badly about what you do. Let's imagine that this magic pill allows you to look good even if you are acting badly. The pill makes you a master at managing your image— you can do whatever you want and blame everyone else. Let's imagine that you win most arguments. Let's imagine that other people are happy to take care of your problems so they can feel needed. Let's imagine that you always get the best end of the deal, and other people are happy and willing to do the work of the relationship. Let's imagine you looking at others as if they are your puppets. Let's imagine that the pill allows you to use your anger, your threats, your secrets, or your silence to get others to do what you want. The magic pill allows you to be as selfish as you want and go after what you want. You never have to take responsibility, and you never feel remorseful. The pill shows you how to say just the right thing to get people to change their behavior in order to make you happy.

If you had that kind of power and control over another person or other people, consider for a moment what it would take for you to stop taking that pill?

Toxic people's behavior is a problem for you, but it's foolish to assume that their behavior is a problem for *them*. If their behavior weren't working for them, they would change it. Toxic people change tactics. They change approaches. They change how they make you feel on a given day. But they rarely change into a less selfish version of themselves. If they wanted to change overall, they would.

If you have tried to talk someone into getting help and they refused to get help, this only serves as further proof that they know what they are doing. "We need to learn to communicate better!" you plead. "We need to learn to work together! Let's get help. Let's talk to someone. I'm here for you!" You can only imagine their point of view when someone tells them they need to change or get help. They are already getting their way. Why would they change? They ask themselves, "Why would I give up my solution to life's problems? I get to behave badly, and you still think I am good. I get my way, appear to be the good girl/guy, and get you to do the work of the relationship. You want me to give that up? I've figured out the secret to life. You are just mad because you aren't as good at the game as I am."

> "What our intuition tells us a manipulator is really like challenges everything we've been taught to believe about human nature. We've been inundated with a psychology that has us viewing people with problems, at least to some degree, as afraid, insecure or "hung-up." So, while our gut tells us we're dealing with a ruthless conniver, our head tells us they must be really frightened, wounded, or self-doubting 'underneath.' What's more, most of us generally hate to think of ourselves as callous and insensitive

people. We hesitate to make harsh or negative judgments about others. We want to give them the benefit of the doubt and believe they don't really harbor the malevolent intentions we suspect. We're more apt to doubt and blame ourselves for daring to believe what our gut tells us about our manipulator's character."

—George K. Simon Jr., *In Sheep's Clothing: Understanding and Dealing With Manipulative People*

People who are Toxic Person Proof™ know that patterns count, and promises don't. People who are Toxic Person Proof™ know that if a toxic person really wanted to change, they would be making *long-term* sustainable efforts to do so. An apology without changed behavior is just manipulation.

A SECRET TO HELPING YOU KNOW IF SOMEONE KNOWS WHAT HE OR SHE IS DOING

It may be tempting to believe a person can't help themselves from exhibiting toxic behaviors. One way to figure out if he knows what he is doing is to reflect on how he acts in different circumstances. It is rare for a toxic person to act like a beast in public and an angel in private. Toxic people know who they can act badly in front of without ruining their game. They know when they need to change their behavior to keep their image as the victim or the hero of any given situation.

Have you ever had someone yell at you while you were both in the car, and then completely change their demeanor when the two of you got out of the car? They know what they are doing. Have you ever asked yourself, "Why is he so nice to everyone else and so mean to me? He knows what he is doing. Have you ever noticed the fact that she always seems to have a crisis right before you have a big event coming up? It's as though she can't handle a day being about anything other than her? She knows what she is doing.

Knowing how to act in public versus how to act in private makes it clear that someone is using anger, pouting, or crisis to get their way. It doesn't mean they are stressed or lonely or need more care and attention. It means they are manipulating you, plain and simple. They are using bad behavior to get the upper hand in a situation. This is obviously a problem for you, but to a toxic person, their manipulation is a solution. Toxic behavior is how they get their way. They use their bad behavior to avoid taking responsibility, growing up, working hard, being vulnerable, or being seen for who they really are.

I want to point out this again:

A predictable pattern of using one's bad behavior through tactics such as the silent treatment, anger, blame- shifting, or putting you on defense in order to get the upper hand in a situation is a problem, but it is only a problem for you. To the other person, it's a solution. And it is a solution they draw upon often. A solution they KNOW they can use to get what they want and avoid what they don't want.

RECOGNIZE YOUR EMOTIONAL TIES TO THE OUTCOME

The more emotionally connected you are to someone not being toxic, the more likely you are to miss the fact that they are.

The biggest reason why a red flag list isn't enough to grab our attention is that we don't want people we know and love to be toxic. No one wants a toxic mother, brother, boss, aunt, cousin, boyfriend, or wife. No one wants to enter into a toxic situation, nor do they want to miss a potential opportunity. People miss signs of toxicity because they really, really, *want* the situation not to be toxic. They want the toxic person's words to be true. They were emotionally connected to the outcome, so they are willing to ignore their observations. This is why you see people in horrible situations who don't realize they are having a toxic person encounter. They tell themselves they aren't having a toxic person encounter. This is also the reason why it is easier to notice other people's toxic person encounters while missing our own.

See if you have noticed the following pattern:

1. Someone has a toxic person encounter.
2. They study toxic people.
3. They assume that since they now can make a list of red flags, they are Toxic Person Proof™.
4. They are quick to point out toxic people who affect other people's lives.
5. They miss toxic person encounters in their own life.

"I can't believe she is putting up with that. If someone ever treated me like that, I would show him what's up. His clothes would be all over the yard, and I would have his face on a billboard with a huge WARNING sign."

—Beth

It is easy to know exactly what play the coach should have called to win the game from the comfort of your living room without the pressure of the screaming fans. Similarly, it is easier to say what we would do in toxic situations that we are not actually in. This is difficult for the person hoping to get empathy and understanding from a friend or family member and conveniently allows us to maximize why other people should not put up with toxic behavior and minimize the toxic behaviors we ourselves put up with. It is also comforting to tell ourselves that because we can spot other people's toxic person encounters, we are able to protect ourselves from our own toxic person encounters.

Understanding what toxic people do is not the same as being Toxic Person Proof™. If we are emotionally connected to the outcome, we are more likely to have blind spots. This isn't because we don't understand what it means to be toxic. It's because we are emotionally connected to the person or situation not being toxic.

A common theme I hear over and over is, "I think I'm Toxic Person Proof™ because I can spot other people putting up with toxic behavior." People with toxic parents talk badly about people in toxic business partnerships. People with toxic business partnerships feel superior to people in toxic romantic relationships. People in toxic romantic relationships point out parents who need to have better boundaries with manipulative children. Our own toxic person encounter is "not a big deal," but others should really do something about *their* toxic person encounter. This type of thinking blinds us to the toxic people in our own lives. It makes for a big win for toxic people hoping to manipulate and a big, fat loss for us.

LESSONS FROM A HOT DOG

I want you to imagine a hot dog—all pink and wiggly and full of chemicals, just happily engulfing a skewer without the confines of a bun. You can roll that hot dog around and see every inch of its juicy pink deliciousness. Now imagine how much less of the pink skin you see when you put it in a bun. You can only catch a glimpse of the pink. The main thing you see is the bread.

Your logical brain is the hot dog all by itself. It isn't encumbered by emotions, and you have full access to every nook and cranny. When you see other people's toxic person problems, you have full access to your logical brain. When you're emotionally attached to the outcome, you put your logical brain inside the emotional bun. You can't get to the logic because it's wrapped up in emotion. When you are looking in on someone else's life, you are not as emotionally connected. You can lead with logic. When it's your life, however, or your relationship, job, or sister, your logical brain goes inside your emotional bun. Your logical brain is still there, of course, but you can't access it as easily because it is encased by your emotions in the same way that a bun encases a hot dog.

This is why understanding toxic behaviors aren't the same as being Toxic Person Proof™. Don't get me wrong, being able to point out toxicity in other people's lives is an amazing first step! Yet truly being Toxic Person Proof™ involves being mindful of the fact that it is easier to see what someone else should do than to see what we should do. We are not emotionally connected to their problems, their lives, and their relationships in the same way we are connected to our own lives, our own problems, and our own relationships. We, therefore, give advice we don't take ourselves and advise others to fix problems we don't see in our own lives. We subconsciously know it's easier to see the toxic behavior other people should confront than see the toxic behavior we should confront. We maximize their toxic person problems and minimize our own toxic person problems. And then, we fall into optimism bias and tell ourselves we are Toxic Person Proof™, and the beat goes on and on and on. Toxic people keep winning, and we keep telling ourselves it isn't happening. We are fine. Life is fine.

There is a Bible verse that says, "Why do you look at the speck of sawdust in your brother's eye while ignoring the plank in your own eye?" This verse has wisdom for all of us who wish to become Toxic Person Proof™. "Why do you look at the toxic people in other's lives while ignoring the toxic behavior you are putting up with in your own life?" Most of us could benefit from a little eyeball cleaning.

I cannot emphasize enough that this is why studying lists of red flags or personality disorders is not enough. Look at the plank in your own eye. Look at the people currently using you. What red flags are you telling yourself are not really red? What facts are you ignoring because they are too painful to confront? What would your logical brain know if you stopped covering it up with emotion? What are you covering up because you don't want it to be true? What hope are you clinging to when the data say something else?

Summary: Toxic people know what they are doing. The more emotionally connected you are to someone not being toxic, the more likely you are to miss their toxic behaviors.

Of the areas covered, which is the biggest struggle for you? Do you find yourself being able to spot toxic person encounters in other people's lives while ignoring the toxic behaviors in your own life? Do you give in to emotion and ignore the information you gather from your observations? Give yourself the gift of ten minutes to really reflect on what areas you need to strengthen to become Toxic Person Proof™.

CHAPTER 4

UNCOVERING YOUR BLINDSPOTS

"We all have a blind spot and it's shaped exactly like us."
—Junot Diaz

There are so many things I am grateful for in life: clean water, strong coffee, the ability to live every day on purpose, deep friendships, the love of a good man, and tacos, just to name a few. But my gratitude for one thing surpasses nearly everything else, and I can't imagine living without it. I take it with me everywhere I go, and without it I am utterly and completely lost.

I love you, GPS. I love you and I don't care who knows it!

My sense of direction (or rather, lack thereof) is terrifying. There is a quote often attributed to Einstein that says, "If you judge a fish by its ability to climb a tree, it will live its whole life believing that it's stupid." If you judged my intelligence by my sense of direction, you would think *I* was stupid. As a kid, I spent car rides with my head in a book like a good little nerd, while my sister wisely looked around to figure out where we were going. The result? I can rock standardized testing, but when I was sixteen, I couldn't figure out how to get to my grandmother's house. Mind you, this was the house my father grew up in, the house that was only fifteen minutes away from my own childhood home.

Before GPS, my friends and family had become used to me showing up to events both late and crying. Actually, truth be told, even *with* GPS, I show up to events late and crying. But not *as* late. And without as *much* crying.

People try to help. "Do you know which direction Northwest is?"

"No."

"Do you know where Baker Street is?'

"Nope."

"Do you know where the park is?"

"No."

"Do you know where your car is?"

Also no.

"What? Are you serious? How are you going to find the car?" they ask me with concern in their eyes.

"Easy," I reply. "I just push the panic button and then move toward the sound. Works every time!" This approach seems to bother everyone else much more than it bothers me.

I'm sure that three hundred years ago, this lack of directional ability would have been a huge hindrance to my survival. Luckily, because of GPS I don't have to be Sacagawea. I can just plug in my coordinates and hope my phone battery doesn't die before I arrive wherever I'm going.

I know my sense of direction is something I have to be aware of, something I have to plan and prepare for. Throughout the years, I have also realized that I need to have a better plan to avoid toxic person encounters. I need to prepare and be aware of the blind spots that make me vulnerable. I've learned that I have to be humble enough to admit that when I am emotionally connected to a situation, then I am more likely to have blind spots than I am when I'm not emotionally connected to the situation.

For example, I would be less likely to ignore the red flags on a job interview if I didn't need the job. I'm less likely to put up with toxic behavior from a friend if I have lots of friends. I am more likely to ignore red flags in my own family than I would be to ignore red flags in someone else's family. I am human. Accepting that I am a vulnerable human actually protects me from being vulnerable.

Becoming Toxic Person Proof™ requires knowing I need a GPS system to keep my logical mind engaged, even if I am emotionally connected to the outcome of a situation. Becoming Toxic Person Proof™ requires knowing I need a GPS system so that I don't make excuses for ignoring the red flags. Becoming Toxic Person Proof™ requires that I recognize my blind spots.

TOXIC PEOPLE KNOW OUR BLIND SPOTS BETTER THAN WE DO

I can choose to ignore my blind spots or pretend I am super-human, but this makes me more likely to fall prey to a toxic person. Being Toxic Person Proof™ requires that we recognize that toxic people have gathered information about us.

So, what do toxic people know that we don't?

- They know how to recognize the weaknesses of people who think they would never fall for a toxic person encounter.
- They know how often we are willing to assume positive intent.
- They know how often we are willing to keep trying to help.
- They know we will default to believing them rather than admitting to ourselves that we were wrong about them.
- They know we are likely to mistake great chemistry for great character.
- They know we are likely to mistake being a successful person for being a safe person.
- They know we are likely to assume they didn't mean to behave badly.
- They know how often we are willing to accept blame to preserve relationships.
- They know how often we are willing to take ownership for problems within the relationship or situation.
- They know how often we are willing to choose moving on over being right (which means they get to be right every dang time!).

Toxic people probably know your blind spots better than you do. Toxic people know we all see from our own eyes, our own characters, our own belief systems, our own points of integrity. Toxic people know that the less toxic we are, the less likely we are to pick up on their toxic games. If you have been duped by a toxic person, take comfort in the fact that you can forgive yourself. I know you probably aren't particularly grateful that you fell for their games, but the good news is, the fact that you didn't see and understand the behavior means that you are not toxic! There are games toxic people play and things they understand about society and human psychology that most of us don't. They require this understanding in order to survive and thrive.

15 Common Blind Spots

Blindspot #1: I Am Safe From Toxic Person Encounters.

"There is no way I could get tricked. I would totally see it coming and not put up with that crap."

"I've been tricked by a toxic person before, so there is no way it could happen again because I've done my research on personality disorders and mental illness. I am practically a narcissist expert!"

"Toxic person encounters don't happen to people like me. I'm sure I'm safe."

Do you consider yourself an above-average driver? Eight out of ten people do[1]. Since eight out of ten people can't all be above average, there are those among us who are lying to ourselves. Those among us who are telling ourselves we could never have a toxic person encounter are also lying to ourselves (which, incidentally, makes us more likely to have a toxic person encounter rather than less likely). We call this optimism bias—maintaining the notion that bad things aren't going to happen to us. They might happen to other people, but they won't happen to me. They might be able to trick other people, but they can't trick me.

My guess is that you have overcome optimism bias in other areas of your life. You probably realize that you should wear your seatbelt because you aren't exempt from the risk of car wrecks. You probably know to wear sunscreen if you want to avoid skin cancer. You probably know not to use the same password for dogbones.com and yourbankaccount.com You probably put on a helmet when you ride your motorcycle, going exactly the speed limit with the wind in your face and bugs in your teeth as you jam out to "Free Bird". In short, you know you are not immune to the dangers of life in other areas. It's time to recognize that you aren't immune to a toxic person encounter either. We become safer when we realize people do get sick. Bad things can happen to each and every one of us. And toxic people really do exist.

My experience with optimism bias came from thinking I could earn the right to be Toxic Person Proof™ rather than learn how to become Toxic Person Proof™. This was a huge blind spot in my own life. I tried to be annoyingly good to avoid bad things happening to me. I thought I could avoid toxic person tragedy by pouring kindness and good deeds into the world. I chose to spend my Spring Break feeding the orpans instead of partying like a rock star. I chose to serve and pray and give and give some more. I know that a part of me thought I could be so good that life would protect me. That I could pour so much good karma into the world that I could be Toxic Person Proof™ without worrying about the data or actually learning to become Toxic Person Proof™. That I could be so good to others that God would be good to me.

I thought I could have so many people's backs that the Universe would have mine. I wanted to do good work so that I didn't have to do the work of protecting myself. I thought I could earn life's protection. You can imagine how unsuccessful I was. I didn't write this book because that strategy worked.

Looking back, I realize that my strategy involved doing the same thing over and over while hoping to get different results. I kept thinking I needed to use different words so people could hear me. I tried to be less selfish, more patient, more giving, and more forgiving. I missed the realities of people treating me badly over and over and over and kept getting in toxic situation after toxic situation after toxic situation. I finally realized this one simple truth:

Dear Sarah,

If it isn't working, stop doing it.

Love,
Sarah

What I wanted to work: Keep getting better at the things I was already good at. Be even more nice so others were nice back. Bargain with God, the Universe, and anyone and everyone who would listen.

What actually worked: Getting better at what I was bad at—things like tapping into wisdom and intuition when meeting someone new, and seeing who people are rather than who I hoped they would be. Things like being a peacemaker rather than a peacekeeper. Things like recognizing that sometimes people are mean on purpose. Recognizing there are people who are looking to trick me on purpose, use my kindness against me, and always gain the upper-hand position in our interactions. Things like recognizing that people are who they choose to be rather than assuming that everyone wants to be better, and that with a little bit of my magic love and fairy dust, I could make them into the version of themselves I think they should be.

I had to recognize my blind spots because the toxic people in my life certainly recognized them! And they continued to use them against me. I was telling myself that I could never have a toxic person encounter, that toxic people didn't exist, that they couldn't trick me, or that the Universe would protect me. I had to learn to work to avoid assholes in the same way I work to avoid potholes.

We avoid potholes because we realize that potholes exist and we need to watch out for them. We don't assume that our cars will magically know what to do when we encounter a pothole simply because we are good people. We don't tell ourselves that God will protect us and magically cover up the pothole before our car glides across it. We watch out for potholes because we want to protect ourselves from a flat tire. We would do well to approach assholes the same way.

We need to recognize that there are assholes out there, and we need to watch out for them. We need to plan for them rather than tell ourselves we will be able to swerve at the last minute. We need to know we have some responsibility for protecting ourselves rather than hoping it all magically works out. Thinking we don't need a plan is a blind spot that works to a toxic person's advantage rather than our own.

Blind Spot #2: I'm Too Tired to Give Up Now. I'll Be Strong Later.

Throughout humanity, we have been blessed with great minds who used what they knew to shape the future of humanity. People like Aristotle, Galileo, Leonardo, Dickens, and Newton changed our futures forever. The geniuses of yesteryear gave us masterpieces that we can gaze at for centuries and stories that taught us what it means to be living. They also cured polio which was pretty cool. The geniuses of today give us endless opportunities to stare at screens and give us stories to help us forget about our lives (or cure boredom).

"Show starting in five seconds."

"Don't miss the next episode."

"Next game loading."

"You have a new notification."

Today's tech geniuses and giants do it on purpose. It's an endless fight for our attention. "Stay with me a little longer. Just one more episode," our screens sing to us. "One more game, one more show, one more hour. Don't give up on me yet." We love the lure of this love song, and we go toward the light like the sirens of the Odyssey.

It's rarely a good decision to give another hour of our lives away to the kings of screens, entertainment, and social media, but we do it anyway. It seems easier to give the screen what it wants because, secretly, it's what we want. I'll finish the report later, get to the homework later, catch up on my sleep later, exercise later, spend time with my children later. I'm so tired...it's just easier to give technology another chance.

I'm so tired. It's easier to give him (or her) another chance.

Toxic people use this same song to keep us in the game of toxic person encounters as well. "Stay with me a little longer. Just one more time," our toxic person sings to us.

"One more game, one more show, one more hour. Don't give up on me yet!" Toxic people know how much effort it requires for you to escape a toxic person encounter. They know how much easier it is for you to tell yourself, "I'll figure it out next week. I'll worry about it later." It seems easier to give the screen what it wants, because secretly it's what *we* want. If you want to be Toxic Person Proof™, it is critical to recognize when this is happening. Staying in a toxic situation longer does not give you more energy. Use your energy to help you, not to make excuses to stay in a relationship with a toxic person.

Blind Spot #3: Time Will Fix This

"I'll just hope for the best and dismiss the bad behavior in hopes that it will get better."

"Just because she did it today doesn't mean she'll do it tomorrow."

"*All* men are like this; sometimes you just have to deal with it. Just make yourself busy with work, and it will get better."

"It will be better after he retires."

One of the biggest benefits that blind spots provide to toxic people is the amount of power we give to the concept of time. We tell ourselves that time will heal all wounds. We make time the ultimate medicine, fairy godmother, and prayer answerer. We make time the magic bullet that will save us. We tell ourselves that good things come to those who wait.

Yet, the only thing time promises us is that it will pass. We will get older. Time will keep ticking. Days will turn into weeks, which will turn into months, which will turn into years. What we decide to do with that time and what others choose to do with that time is the reason things change. Far too often, we miss that our choices and actions over the course of time do not make things better. Things don't just get better because the hands on the clock move. Hoping things will magically work out just because time passes is a strategy that works for toxic people much more effectively than it will ever work for you. They convince you to give up years of your life to hope and promises, because that way, they do not have to change their behavior.

Blind Spot #4: I've Invested Too Much to Give Up Now

"I have already given up half of my life. How can I give up on half my life without a fight?"

"I'm giving him the benefit of the doubt. I believed all his excuses. I kept thinking I'm too far in to let this get to me, and I believe that things will get better."

Not only do we tell ourselves that time will magically solve our problems, we also tell ourselves that already having wasted years in the past is a good reason to waste years in the future. The most dangerous thing about telling yourself that things will get better with time is that the more time you give to a situation, the more time you have invested into the situation. This is one of the reasons it is so important to train yourself to walk away from toxic situations much earlier. If you have given up three years of your life, it is more difficult to admit "failure" than if you had given up three weeks. If you have given up three *decades* to a toxic person encounter, it becomes even more difficult!

Unfortunately, this is a blind spot that will only keep you stuck! The more time you have given, the less likely the situation is to change, not vice versa. If the hole is deep, stop digging! The best time to plant a tree was ten years ago, and the next best time is today. If you decide to keep going on the same path, you will likely wake up a year from now with the same life. If, however, you decide to change paths, a year will still pass. The difference is that you will have a chance at making your life better.

If you or someone you care about is thinking, "I've already given up five years," flip it around and ask, "are you planning on giving it another five years?" When we are stuck in the muck of thinking, we have to remind ourselves that time is going to pass either way. Changing what we do with our time is a much better strategy than giving more time to something we already know doesn't work.

Blind Spot #5: I Am Probably the Problem

"I told myself I wasn't perfect either."
    "I told myself I was overreacting."
    "I thought, 'I caused this. I did this to myself.'"
    "It's my paranoia, it's not real."
    "I told myself I was being too needy, too sensitive."
    "She wasn't trying to be mean. I'm just too sensitive about things."
    "He loves me. I'm being too emotional."
    "I wasn't trying/working hard enough."
    One of the reasons why wonderful people end up having toxic person encounters is because they are self-reflective and willing to take more than their fair share of responsibility for the problems in the relationship. The concern rises when they get so focused on fixing themselves that they miss the problems the other person brings to the situation.

It's the coworker who is willing to "own up" to his part of the disagreement in front of the boss. He wants to act in his own integrity and admit to himself and others that he is not perfect. This trait is amazing when both parties are willing to admit fault. It is detrimental in a toxic person encounter. In your efforts to admit your faults and work on your problems, the dynamic quickly flips, and you become the only problem. The toxic person places the blame on you, you continue to blame and work on yourself, and the toxic person avoids any and all responsibility. This becomes exhausting after weeks, months, and years.

Toxic people also use the blind spot to keep your eyes on you and off of them. Counselors, teachers and religious leaders enforce the need to "just worry about changing you. Don't worry about changing someone else." Trying to do the right thing, you work on being less sensitive, less reactive, less bothered, less needy, and less upset when someone else behaves badly. This strategy works for the toxic person because you are working on yourself rather than noticing how many of the problems stem from the toxic person's behavior. Plus, the toxic person is *thrilled* that you are getting better at putting up with their bad behavior. You end up doing all the work, and the toxic person reaps all the reward. Yet, people who are self-reflective and willing to work on themselves completely miss this! In fact, they think they are doing the right thing. To become Toxic Person Proof™, we must recognize when this is happening, when our self-responsibility and willingness to work on ourselves is being used against us.

Blind Spot #6: No One Is Perfect

"All relationships have problems."

"No workplace is perfect."

"We were both broken, and it will get better."

"I told myself my expectations were too high and what I really wanted was a fantasy."

If you find yourself in a toxic person encounter, one of the biggest comforts found in telling yourself that no one and nothing is perfect. This means you can work on lowering your expectations rather than asking the other person to raise the standards of their behavior. Once again, you end up doing all the work of the relationship. To overcome this blind spot, think about your life as a TV show. Would it be a drama? How would people view your character? Would they think you were ridiculous for putting up with whatever you were putting up with? Would they see you as the brunt of the jokes? Would they see you as a doormat? What decisions would the viewers want to see you make? Nothing and no one is perfect, but this blind spot can lead you into talking yourself into cognitive dissonance and to ignoring what is really happening in your life.

Blind Spot #7: Everyone Deserves the Benefit of The Doubt

I remember talking to a woman who said things were only good five percent of the time within her relationship. Yet she kept telling me that it was the "real" him who was good during that five percent of the time—that the harmful version of him who appeared ninety-five percent of the time was not the "real" him. This woman had built businesses and obtained a medical degree. She was far from dumb. She just happened to be hoping for things that had no basis in reality. She wanted to believe in the best rather than believe in the data. Unfortunately, the data was clear. The pattern had a consistent skew, and that skew did not lean toward the "real" him being good to her.

In the book *When To Walk Away*, Gary Thomas described the faith journey he took as he learned to identify toxic people. At first, he felt badly assuming that anyone had bad intentions. But he then realized how immature it was to assume that no one ever acted badly. Thomas realized he was avoiding the crucial process of learning discernment and spiritually bypassing the important work of figuring out who was safe for him to be around. When we want to avoid figuring out who someone really is, it is easy to tell ourselves that we are being kind by giving people the benefit of the doubt, but Thomas points out that it isn't kind. It is actually immature and irresponsible.

Becoming Toxic Person Proof™ does represent spiritual, mental, and emotional growth. It requires that you go deeper and use the power of thinking (not overthinking!) to keep yourself safe. Don't let giving people the benefit of the doubt be the blind spot that allows toxic people to slip into your life undetected. Keep believing in the good! Just believe that there are different types of people in the world, and it is your job to figure out who is who.

Blind Spot #8: This Isn't Who He or She Really Is

"That wasn't the REAL Kim. This was the mid-life crisis Kim. The alcoholic Kim. The hurting Kim. The redeemable Kim. The REAL Kim was the woman who pursued me for seven years before we ever dated. The REAL Kim was the woman I saw on our wedding day. The REAL Kim was the person I saw in the positive moments. That is what I believed."

In the last several years I have heard hundreds of men and women tell me stories about toxic people having two sides to their personality. In some moments Kim is wonderful to be around. In other moments the mask falls off and the toxic behavior begins. Toxic people are fabulous at image management. It is common knowledge that there are two sides to every story, and we will be better off as a society once we realize that there are two sides to toxic people—which is precisely why we can't believe their stories.

This dualistic nature of their personalities leaves us trying to figure out who they really are. It is comforting to tell ourselves that the nice version of them is the "real" version of them, and we just need to help get them back to that "real" version of themselves. If we figure out the problem, the "why" of their behavior, things will go back to "normal."

"I told myself he was stressed out with his career."

"I made excuses for her because her job was so hard."

"If I get him the right help, he will change."

The theme becomes one wherein one person is trying to figure the toxic person out and make excuses for bad behavior. Work stress is the problem. Home stress is the problem. Alcohol is the problem. A bad childhood is the problem. Notice that everything is a problem except for the toxic person's behavior.

This is a major blind spot in two ways. First, you end up doing all the work of trying to figure out the real problem without realizing that the toxic person's choice to treat you badly *is* the real problem. Second, you tell yourself that the "real" version of the toxic person is kind, patient, loving, good, responsible, and honest. This version of them isn't the real person. The disruptive, angry, moody, silent, lazy, irresponsible, avoidant version of them is simply a result of the "real" problem.

You can't get to California using a map that only takes you to Florida. You cannot get a law degree by applying to medical schools. You can't work on your biceps by studying calf raises. If you want to solve your problems, the first step is figuring out the specific problem you are trying to solve. Toxic people do not want you to figure out the specific problem. Your confusion makes you easier to control. Telling yourself that "this isn't who she really is" is a blind spot that keeps you confused.

Open yourself up to the possibility that someone's choices make up who they are. Someone's pattern of behavior tells the world whether or not they are safe to be around. Everyone has bad days. Not everyone has bad patterns. Figure out who a person really is by the patterns of his or her behavior rather than trying to figure out the problem. Hint: their behavior IS the problem!

Blind Spot #9: They Are Full of Potential

There is a reason people say, "Don't fall in love with potential." Putting too much emphasis on someone's potential is one of the most prominent reasons why we avoid seeing red flags. We tell ourselves, "This is who they are now, but this is not who they will be later."

Why do we do that?

It is easy to forget that people in their early twenties have potential, but grown adults have patterns. Look for the patterns, not the potential. See who someone is rather than who you hope he or she will become. People with a pattern of success continue with a pattern of success ninety-nine percent of the time. People with a pattern of problems continue with a pattern of problems ninety-nine percent of the time. If you are holding onto the one percent hope that they will change, I recommend that you bet on a Roulette wheel in Vegas over betting on someone's potential to transform into a different person. Falling in love with potential is great if what you want to fix up is a house, but it's horrible if what you want to fix up is a person.

There are stories of people who have potential and go on to create great lives. However, sticking by a toxic person who has potential rarely earns you the loyalty you hope to gain. I have heard both business leaders and romantic partners take on someone who has potential, helping them to build up their life. You know what the toxic person does after they grow into their full potential? They leave the people who took a chance on them in the first place.

Blind Spot #10: But It Isn't All Bad

"I kept thinking we could go back to the way things were at the beginning. I just kept hoping that part was real, and we could get back there to that happiness. But it was all fake."

"He isn't disrespectful all the time. No one is perfect. Now I know it was intermittent reinforcement with a good case of trauma bond. Glad those days are over."

If the toxic person encounter was one hundred percent bad, you would walk away from the toxic person more easily. This is why toxic people have to make things good sometimes—so you don't walk away. Don't let this be a blind spot. Notice how often they are "nice" when they want something. You are not a dog that accepts treats every time someone wants you back. Don't let this blind spot allow another person the opportunity to train you to put up with more bad behavior.

An apology without change is simply more manipulation. An "I love you" is not the same as an "I was wrong." Doing something nice for you or planning something fun is not the same as being less selfish. Changed behavior equals someone actually changing. Promises alone mean nothing. Dropping in some good behavior in order to distract you from bad behavior is not the same as changing. Becoming Toxic Person Proof™ requires that you see the whole picture, not just maximize the good times and minimize the bad times.

Keeping a calendar and taking quick notes each day can be helpful in overcoming this blind spot. Do you see a pattern of good behavior? A pattern of difficult behavior? A pattern of throwing in something good to distract you when they are mistreating you? Focus on the pattern rather than the promises! If they really want to change, they will actually change.

Blind Spot #11: I Am the Only One Who Really Knows Them

"When someone else warned me, I thought they just didn't know him well enough."

"I thought God had changed her."

If people are seeing things you are not, it is because they aren't as emotionally engaged as you are in ensuring that the relationship continues. If you notice yourself with blind spots such as "I'm the only one who really knows him," please keep track of how many people are warning you and what they are saying. It is extremely likely that you are seeing a masked up, manipulative version of the toxic person. It is the basis of almost all love stories to be the only one who understands one's partner. It is the basis of almost all nightmares to end up thinking you know a person, begin defending that person, and then realizing that everyone else was actually right.

Blind Spot #12: Other People Trust Them

"He was my childhood best friend, so I kept telling myself that he'd NEVER do that to me!"

The powerful military general. The religious leader. The teacher. The start-up guru on the cover of *Fortune* magazine. Just because other people trust someone doesn't make that person trustworthy. Being successful isn't the same thing as being honest! Just look at all the corrupt leaders or powerful people in history.

Remember, "There are toxic people, and you know them." Don't put on blinders and assume that all the corrupt leaders are people I don't know, while all the honest and moral leaders are people I do know. Don't assume that everyone other than you is Toxic Person Proof™ either. Throughout history, groups have been fooled time and time again. Don't allow "group think" to do your thinking for you. Just because friends and family members know of a person does not necessarily mean they know the true integrity of that person.

Blind Spot #13: I Am Special

"I thought I was the special one and different from all the others."

"I can fix this!" was always my thought.

"They just never had anyone truly love them. I can show them what real love is like."

This has got to be one of the most overlooked blind spots that toxic people use to keep others trapped. If a toxic person wants to use you, he or she will at first make you feel special. It feels great to be selected, singled out, and sought out! It can make you feel as if you are chosen. No one wants to go from feeling chosen to feeling discarded, so when this happens, you instantly find yourself working to remain special without realizing you are actually working to earn your place in the relationship.

Caregivers are vulnerable to this because they believe that loving well is their greatest strength. They hope their love alone will be enough and miss the fact that a lack of love is not the problem. The toxic person's behavior is the problem. Caregivers hope to give love while hoping that the love given will make the person with toxic behavior want to change. The person with toxic behavior, meanwhile, wants to keep the caregiver thinking that they need to give more love rather than more consequences. Eventually, the caregiver's blind spot will result in him or her being used by toxic person after toxic person.

People who are Toxic Person Proof™ know they are not God. They are not all-powerful. They are not magicians. They are not fairy godmothers. They are not magic pill makers. They may be special, but they cannot be so special that they can change the personality of those around them. Toxic Person Proof™ people see specific behavior and immediately believe it reflects who the other person is. They don't lie to themselves and say, "But after my special love, just think about who he or she could be!" Remember, don't fall in love with potential. Your love and specialness are not the missing links. Their desire to get better is the missing link.

> "The bottom line in both cases is that people don't change; that no matter how charming you are and how fiercely you love, you cannot turn a person into something she's not."
> —Jodi Picoult

Blind Spot #14: Hurt People Hurt People

"She had a tough childhood."

Does having a hurtful past give someone a pass to hurt others? Do you think people who have been hurt should be able to hurt others? When you hurt, do you think that is an excuse to hurt others?

My guess is that if you are a good, kind, loving, giving person, you try to find other ways to manage your hurt rather than giving yourself permission to hurt others in response. We have all had hurtful things happen to us, and those among us who are more mature try to get the help we need in order to create the life and relationships we want.

Toxic people, however, play the victim instead, often using their past as an excuse to hurt other people. Don't allow this blind spot to open the door that allows someone to use your kindness against you. Furthermore, remember the importance of looking for patterns. Helping someone out who is having a hard time is kind. Bailing someone out of their consistent pattern of problems isn't kind or helpful—to you or to them. If you want to support them, give them resources from which they can get help, and then make it their responsibility to get that help. No one can force another person to become a better person. We all have to do our own work.

"ACCEPT NO EXCUSES. Don't buy into any of the many reasons (rationalizations) someone may offer for aggressive, covertly aggressive behavior, or any other inappropriate behavior. If someone's behavior is wrong or harmful, the rationale they offer is totally irrelevant. The ends never justify the means. So, no matter how much an 'explanation' for a problem behavior seems to make sense, don't accept it." - George K. Simon Jr., *In Sheep's Clothing: Understanding and Dealing With Manipulative People*

Blind Spot #15: She Isn't A Bad Person Underneath

"I witnessed him condescend the people he bought building materials from. I was always taken back and embarrassed, but he would blow it off by telling me he was 'not a morning person and needed his coffee.'"

There is a phrase that says, "The eyes are the window to the soul." I disagree. I believe someone's pattern of actions is the window to their soul.

Who someone truly is shows itself over a pattern of time. To become Toxic Person Proof™, we need to look at people's actions to decide whether or not they are safe for us to be around. We all have innate value as humans, but we do not all add equal value to others' lives. There are some people I can choose to be around who will help me strive to be the best version of myself. There are also some people I can choose to be around who are encouraging. Further, there are some people I can choose to be around who frustrate me. There are some people I can choose to be around who are looking for ways to manipulate me and hurt me. While all humans have value, there are some people who will add value to my life more than others.

Before humankind was as transient as we are today, we would judge people by their long-term character rather than by their ability to make a great first impression. When people stayed in the same town with the same people for generation after generation, they were more likely to be viewed according to their actions.

"He's the town drunk," "She's the town gossip," "He's the best guy I know; he pulled my tractor out of the ditch," "She comes from good stock." Then, we started moving more frequently. And when that happened, our first impression became our most important impression. We now hire branding consultants and image consultants and read books on how to make a powerful first impression. You don't need consistency to make a great first impression, but you do need consistency to create a solid frame of character.

Unfortunately, when we meet someone new it is difficult to get an accurate read on their true character. In his book *Talking To Strangers* Malcom Gladwell points out that we tend to believe what people tell us especially when we meet them face to face.[2] Despite Maya Angelou's warning of "When people show you who they are, believe them," we tend to want to default to maximizing the good in people even when we do see signs of toxic behavior. We maximize good actions and minimize bad behavior because we want to believe every person is a good person underneath his or her bad behavior. To become Toxic Person Proof™ we have to develop a new way of thinking about this. It's important to stop asking whether or not someone is good or bad and start questioning whether or not someone is good or bad *for you to be around*. If their actions are showing you who they are, then believe the actions. A great first impression is not the sign of great character. Consistent action is a sign of great character.

"Those who can't change their minds can't change anything."
—George Bernard Shaw

We can only learn from the past if we *actually learn* from the past. If you do not figure out how you lied to yourself before, you will find other ways to lie to yourself. Just because you really, *really* want someone to be different does not, all by itself, make them different. You cannot become Toxic Person Proof™ if you find ways to lie to yourself.

Are you willing to look into warnings others give you?

Are you willing to look at the data rather than the potential?

Are you willing to trust the behavior as the truth?

Summary: Remember, the more emotionally invested you are in someone else not being toxic, the more likely you are to make excuses for their behavior. The more excuses you are willing to make for someone, the more blind spots you are vulnerable to.

Of the fifteen blind spots mentioned, which are the biggest struggle for you? Do you tell yourself the person with toxic behavior does not really mean it when they do or say something unkind? Do you tell yourself that hurt people hurt people? Do you tell yourself that other people would have picked up on it if the person were really toxic? Do you find an excuse to worry about it later? Give yourself the gift of ten minutes, and really reflect on which blind spots you need to strengthen in order to become Toxic Person Proof™.

Chapter 5

Learning the Right Lessons

"Close some doors today. Not because of pride, incapacity or arrogance, but simply because they lead you nowhere."
—Paulo Coelho

We have already discussed why we minimize red flags and overlook blind spots to avoid seeing someone's unhealthy behavior in the last two chapters. But what happens when we do see the truth behind their behavior? Do our brains quickly accept the truth or do our brains still find reasons to stay entangled in the toxic person encounter?

Our brains are meaning-making machines, and when it comes to a toxic person encounter, we can assign some awfully crazy meanings to the reasons we allowed (or are currently allowing) ourselves to be in a toxic relationship. We comfort ourselves with justifications such as "It really helped me learn where my triggers are" or "I learned where I was still selfish" or "This relationship helped me learn how to be alone."

I am sending all the love and snuggles as I say this, but the only lesson you are *supposed* to learn is this: Toxic people hurt your life, and you should stay away from them. When you give toxic people less access to your life, you will have a better life. The less toxic behavior you put up with, the less toxic person encounters you will suffer from. Toxic people suck all the happiness out of the room. They may start out shiny, but they turn out shitty.

Seeing the best in people and creating silver linings from bad situations is a wonderful, fabulous, amazing quality—unless you are having a toxic-person encounter. Toxic people are wonderful, fabulous, and *amazing* at using your positivity to their advantage. You consistently give them another chance, another year, another opportunity. You give them your heart, and your hope becomes bigger than your intelligence. You tell yourself they can change and ignore the signs that they don't want to do so. You tell yourself that you don't let their behavior get to you, and you ignore the signals your body is sending, indicating that they are getting to you. You cling to the sliver of potential and ignore the stacks of data they present at your feet. You know they *could* be better so you comfort yourself with the belief that they *will* be better—if only you put up with their bad behavior for a little bit longer.

STOP MAKING THE BEST OF THINGS

I know that it may seem as though making the best of things is a great quality to have, and it can be—unless toxic people use it against us. Becoming Toxic Person Proof™ means looking for the truth of things rather than just looking for the best of things. Horrible things have happened in history. There have been world wars, sex trafficking, slavery, torture, and deceit, to name but a few.

We try to make the best of things in order to survive the hard parts of our human experience. In many areas of our lives, this quality can be helpful. I know someone who described cancer as having a purpose—and a good one, at that. We need wake-up calls in our lives. Cancer can be one such wake-up call. An affair can be a wake-up call. A social movement can be a wake-up call. A war can be a wake-up call. And a wake-up call can create changes that make our lives or society better.

However, something being deemed a wake-up call doesn't mean that we should romanticize it and create more confusion for ourselves. We can look for the silver lining and try to make the best of cancers, affairs, and wars, but we want less sickness, infidelity, and conflict in our lives. Not more. Putting up with bad behavior from a toxic person in the name of becoming more patient or less selfish is like choosing cancer because you think going through cancer will make you a better person. As meaning-making creatures, we don't want to admit that things are as bad as they are. We look for silver linings without realizing we are desperately trying to survive while telling ourselves we are thriving. We hope for change. We believe the best is yet to come. This is a great trait in many areas of life, but when it comes to toxic people, it is a blind spot that is sure to keep you hooked.

It's not uncommon for me to hear any of the following when working with clients:

"I just really need to work on my patience."

"It's my trust issues."

"This is a great opportunity for me to practice selflessness."

We tell ourselves there is a lesson to learn from our experiences, but far too often, the lesson we are hoping to learn benefits the toxic person much more than it benefits us. There is, however, a lesson we *should* be learning. There are crocodiles out there, and they bite.

Additional forms of distorted thinking I hear:

"But Sarah...I feel like this crocodile is a gift because it allows me to go through life and continually work on healing myself."

"But Sarah...there are only crocodiles out there, so it is best for me to learn to live with the bites."

"But Sarah...being bitten by a crocodile isn't that bad."

"But Sarah...life is hard. Relationships are hard. Everyone is being bitten by crocodiles."

"But Sarah...if I don't allow the crocodile to bite me, then the crocodile will be all alone."

"But Sarah...I am supposed to save the crocodile."

"But Sarah...the crocodile isn't really a crocodile. He is only a crocodile when he has a bad day, doesn't get his way, drinks, wants to cheat on me, wants to scream at me, wants to avoid taking responsibility, wants to look good in front of other people, wants to feel bigger than me, wants me to think he is right, wants to deflect what is really happening. The twenty percent of the time he isn't biting me is the REAL him. The other eighty percent isn't the real him. I have to believe this. I have to keep up hope."

No, you don't. Further, there is not a reward coming for you in exchange for keeping this hope. I know this may be difficult to hear depending on the stage of life you are in. I have never seen anyone hand out a gold star for putting up with bad behavior. No one is going to come in and say, "You did an awesome job putting up with toxic behavior for a long time. You fulfilled your purpose here on earth, which was allowing everyone else to treat you badly. Way to go! It is finally your turn now. You passed the test!"

I know that, on the surface, it might look as though some faith practices appear to reward people who endure toxic person encounters. However, those same faith practices also suggest that it is wrong to help people become better sinners. When you are allowing someone to be as selfish as he or she wants to be and are feeding their addiction to anger, manipulation, blaming, or irresponsibility, that isn't keeping up the faith. That is covering up bad behavior. Helping people behave in worse ways does not equate to being a better Christian/Catholic/Muslim/Jew/Hindu/Buddhist.

Don't allow this blind spot to ruin your life. If you are good at making the best of things, then you can use that same energy to make the *most* of things. You can take the energy you have been expending to survive a life and use that same energy to *create* a life.

I Can Do Hard Things

I am someone who wants things to be fair. I want to be able to work for something and have someone notice my efforts. Maybe it comes from my childhood piano recitals. I practiced for hours, and when I played the song, I wanted people to clap at the end. There have been far too many times in my life when I thought that if I played my cards properly, God would clap at the end. If I helped enough people, I could earn my way to a better life. If

I was selfless enough and kind enough and giving enough and accommodating enough, I could earn my way back to life's favor.

One of the most difficult lessons of my own life has been that I can't earn my way to a Toxic Person Proof™ life with good deeds. I didn't want to stand up for myself; I wanted to be more selfless. I didn't want to create boundaries around my own life; I wanted others to say I deserved to rest because I was doing such a good job. I wanted to save all of the people and help change all of the things. I wanted to stack my good deed cart up so high that I would be crushed by its weight if it toppled over. I thought that if I was that good, maybe I could earn rest. Earn safety. Earn the Universe's protection from toxic people. I thought that if I could do the things I already believed I was good at, I could earn the right not to have to work at the things that didn't feel good.

It didn't work that way. The only way to an easier life was to give myself permission to have an easier life. To stop hiding behind everyone else's problems and face my own.

Ever since my kids were babies, I've had them make "I am" statements. "I am strong. I am brave. I am a critical thinker. I can do hard things." Maybe I gave them the messages I needed to hear when I was their age. It was a season of life wherein I was doing many hard things and making many hard choices that would affect their lives forever.

"Okay, Sarah, you can do hard things" became a mantra. If I was scared, I did it anyway. If it didn't make sense to other people, I did it anyway. If it seemed like I was just looking to change anything until I could change something that actually worked, I did it anyway. Telling myself I can do hard things is an amazing motivator when I need to get away from a toxic situation. But it's a horrible practice when one is in a toxic situation. You can do hard things, yet there is no reward for making it harder.

Telling yourself things like, "Life is supposed to be hard. It will get better. I just need to work harder" is a great way to find yourself in the same place years and years later. There are definitely hard things we have to do in life. However, toxic people make things hard on purpose for their benefit. This will make life much harder, and if the person or situation has been the same for years and years, we are using magical thinking in assuming it will get better on its own.

My dad often says, "If you always do what you have always done, you will always get what you have always gotten." Truly, nothing ever changes without change. And working harder and harder while hoping that the toxic person will eventually decide to change is a strategy that has proven quite ineffective in 99.9 percent of real life.

Yes, our stories and movies and songs tell us most people change for the better with the right amount of time, but adults in their thirties and forties rarely do a 180 to become completely better people in the next decade of life. If they are already grown-ups, they are unlikely to grow into a different person.

I'M STRONG ENOUGH TO TAKE IT

Toxic person encounters require a *lot* of work. Telling yourself you are strong enough to take it requires even *more* work. You try to strengthen yourself, minimize your needs, and lower your expectations. You change so they don't have to. You tell yourself you are strong enough to take it so that you can avoid asking yourself if you *should* be taking it.

The "I am strong enough to take it" belief also shows up when people are trying to develop better boundaries. If you tell yourself that the toxic person problem can be solved with better boundaries, then you can work on *your* boundaries rather than walking away from the toxic person encounter. However, boundaries are about protecting yourself, not changing someone else. Sticking up for yourself isn't a precursor to them changing. Giving someone else a dose of their own medicine won't compel him to stop treating you badly. Trying to teach him a lesson gives him a reason to say that you both are at fault rather than take responsibility for their actions. They are not acting that way because you are not strong enough. They are acting that way because they are getting the better end of the deal.

If you are strong enough to take it, then you are strong enough to change it! You may not be able to change the toxic person, but you can get rid of this blind spot and change *your* future, forever.

Summary: Being strong enough to take it, telling yourself you can do hard things, or trying to learn the wrong lesson can keep you trapped in a toxic situation.

Of the meaning-making blind spots mentioned, which do you struggle with the most? Give yourself the gift of ten minutes, and really reflect on which blind spots you need to strengthen in order to become Toxic Person Proof™. Don't just live a life of creating the best of bad situations. Create a life where you are able to make the most of every experience that comes your way!

CHAPTER 6
UNDERSTANDING SMART-GIRL/GUY SYNDROME

"I Just Need to Work A Little Harder and Hope A Little Longer."

When one grows up being trained as a classical pianist, as I did, she gets used to criticism. It is not a big deal to hear someone tell you that you need to put in an extra two hours of practice one particular week in order to make Beethoven actually sound like Beethoven or to make Rachmaninoff actually sound like Rachmaninoff. Your childhood is spent in rooms with the door closed repeating the same three measures over and over and over again until they are perfect. When your teacher introduces you to a piece of music, you don't expect it to sound like a concert the first time your fingers fumble through the splashes of black notes on the white page. You simply start where you are, put your fingers on the keys, and do your best to make music. Then you do it again. And again. And again. You break it apart, get advice from more advanced musicians, listen, stop, slow down, speed up, and eventually, the song turns into the masterpiece it was meant to be. If it isn't perfect yet, it's no problem. You just have to work a little longer and a little harder.

You may not have grown up playing the piano, but I would guess that there is something in your life you had to work at in order to make it a thing of beauty. Maybe it was your foul shot or your back handspring, your running pace or your sales structure, your marketing plan or your liquid eyeliner (kidding/not kidding for all the women who have left their house after trying to perfect the wingtip and instead ended up looking like they had gotten into a fight with a raccoon. You are not alone in your pain).

Life's journey teaches us that if we want something to improve, we need to work at it. We have to try harder. We have to put in the hours. We have to put in the work. We have to add a little elbow grease. The finish line is getting close. Don't quit now. Quitting is for losers. Good things come to those who wait. Don't stop believing!

Teachers give us gold stars for sticking with it. Coaches reward our hustle. Bosses brag about the employee putting in the extra hours. We get an A for effort. And life trains us to work harder. To get back up when we get kicked down. We tell ourselves we are overcomers. We tell ourselves that this time, things will be different. We keep going, keep up the faith, keep hoping, and keep working to figure it out. Our philosophy of never giving up brings us success. Our philosophy of grit and hustle helps us finally lose the weight, get the raise, start the business, close the deal, make the Dean's List, and transform our music into a masterpiece.

Our philosophy of sticking it out, working harder, and refusing to quit does *not* help us, however, when it comes to toxic person encounters.

Go to a retreat on team building or marriage building, and you will likely hear someone tell you that you need to work harder on your relationships. Yet, talking you into accepting more responsibility for problems in the relationship plays right into a toxic person's strategy. A toxic person may echo the conference leader's or counselor's advice and remind you to work hard, communicate differently, and give up more of yourself. Toxic people tell us we have to forgive—quickly, in fact. Toxic people convince us that "next time will be different." Toxic people tell us we have to hustle. They tell us to put in the extra hours and stop being so selfish, so sensitive. Toxic people tell us to be less of ourselves and keep working to figure it out, to figure *them* out.

And so, we keep trying. Yet it never seems to work. We dedicate ourselves to working even harder! We seek even more outside help. We think, "I may not have the solution, but someone does! I just haven't found the right answer *yet!*" We recruit answers. Human Resources departments tell us we have to learn to work together. Therapists say we have to sacrifice more. Priests suggest that we have to put ourselves last. We read books. We go to retreats. We work on our communication style. We work harder. We try harder. We give more.

It. Is. Never. Enough.

If you are someone who has experienced success in other areas of your life by working harder and not giving up, is it any surprise that you bring that same mindset into a toxic person encounter? One of the hallmarks of a toxic relationship is that one person puts in an enormous amount of work, yet it's never enough to change the relationship. The toxic person has a hole in the bottom of his or her bucket, and your job is to keep pouring. Their mantra seems to be "Give a little bit more." The finish line is always moving, and you are always just short of it.

Hello, smart-girl syndrome, and goodbye, happiness. Smart-girls (or guys) are good at solving problems. They are good at coming up with creative solutions. They are good at overcoming obstacles. They are good at thinking outside the box. They are good at self-reflection and good at developing new skills in order to be successful. They are good at anticipating the needs of others. They are good at sticking with things, even if times are hard right now. They know how to put their feelings aside to get the outcome they want. They know how to adapt and overcome. They know that it's darkest just before dawn, and that if they don't give up now, the sun will come out tomorrow.

Smart-girls/guys are good at turning music into masterpieces. They are good at turning losing games into winning games. They are good at turning chaos into calm, or ashes into beauty. They believe in themselves, and they believe they can help others if only they keep showing up. Smart-girls/guys believe they can be the change they want to see in the world. Smart-girls/guys are not afraid of a little hard work. They know it won't always be easy, and they know that just because things aren't working out *right now* doesn't mean they won't work out in the future. Smart-girls/guys know that they just haven't figured it out *yet*. It doesn't mean they won't figure it out *next*. They don't want to give up because if they do, all the work they've put in will have been for nothing. They don't want to fail. They don't want to give up that easily on people, because part of their identity and happiness is found in being good to people.

We value these qualities in both women and men. We herald good, kind, loving, giving, forgiving, loyal, self-reflective problem solvers. We want to hire these types of people. We want to raise these kinds of children. We want to fill our leadership roles with these types of personalities. Should it be any surprise that toxic people prefer recruiting these personalities as well? Should it be any surprise that someone with tenacity, agreeableness, grit, stamina, kindness, and the willingness to figure things out is the perfect candidate for a toxic relationship?

Still, the story society tells us is that people who've had toxic person encounters were dumb. Broken. Naive. Crazy. Doormats. Gullible. Holders of low self-esteem. Owners of daddy issues. Afraid of conflict. People who fell for toxic work environments were weak. They couldn't stand up for themselves. They couldn't pull themselves up by their bootstraps. People who keep trying to please toxic parents need to get over it. They can't move on. They keep giving away their power.

I understand the confusion that exists when it comes to people who have been in toxic situations. It's probably what I believed at one point in my life too. But it isn't what I believe about toxic person encounters anymore. Are there cases where toxic is drawn to toxic? Sure. Are there cases where needy personalities are drawn to other needy personalities? Of course. Are there cases where people are subconsciously drawn to people who hurt them? Absolutely.

But it isn't always the case. It isn't.

Toxic people are very good at their game. At getting us to believe them. At getting us to help them. At managing their image. At avoiding responsibility. At leaving us a bit confused. We can probably agree with those statements pretty easily at this point. **What is also important to agree on is that toxic people are good at choosing who to be in close relationships with.** In both their personal and professional lives, toxic people want to surround themselves with hopeful, hard-working, self-reflective people who are willing to own their part in their relationships and believe the best about everyone else. Yet far too often, when people have a toxic person encounter, these same good, kind, loving, giving, and forgiving people are led to believe they are dumb, broken, or codependent.

"They seemed so nice at the beginning. When things started going badly, I just assumed it had to be my fault. If I worked harder, things could be better." - Samuel

Samuel was not dumb. **He was trapped in his belief that if something isn't working, you work harder to fix it.** Smart-girl/guy syndrome is the belief that if you are failing at something, you simply need to come up with a different creative solution in order to be successful in that area of life. Unfortunately, when men and women have had toxic person encounters, they aren't informed that they have smart-girl/guy syndrome. They are usually informed that they have codependency issues.

IS IT CODEPENDENCY OR SMART-GIRL/GUY SYNDROME?

Codependency is a buzzword in the area of toxic person encounters. If we are going to help others as well as ourselves, we need to take a closer look at the shocking difference between the definitions of codependency and smart-girl/guy syndrome.

Codependency is characterized by a person who belongs to a dysfunctional, one-sided relationship where one person relies on the other for meeting nearly all of their emotional and self-esteem needs. Codependency is also defined as a relationship that enables another person to maintain their irresponsible, addictive, or under-achieving behavior.

One of the hallmarks of codependency is a lack of self-esteem, and the general idea is that people put up with toxic behavior because they do not have the confidence to walk away from mis-treatment from others. **However, when it comes to smart-girl/guy syndrome, the reason people stay in toxic situations is that they believe in their ability to improve the person or situation with a little hard work. People who believe in themselves and their ability to change are also more likely to believe in the other people's ability to change.** It is, in fact, completely the opposite of having low self-esteem. Smart girls/guys believe in their ability to work hard and improve any situation. They believe in their ability to make any work environment, home, relationship, or friendship better.

"But, Sarah, people seem such a mess after a toxic person encounter. They seem confused and question everything and are emotional. If they are upset after a toxic person encounter, does that mean it's codependency rather than smart-girl/guy syndrome?"

A QUICK TRICK FOR SEEING THE DIFFERENCE IN CODEPENDENCY VERSUS SMART-GIRL/GUY SYNDROME

One of my mother's favorite actresses is Julie Andrews. The hills were certainly alive with the sound of music in my childhood home! When Julie Andrews' character, Maria, was teaching the children how to sing, she said something incredibly important: "Let's start at the very beginning. A very good place to start."

In fact, the very beginning isn't just a very good place to start. It is the ONLY place to start when you are trying to distinguish between codependency and smart-girl/guy syndrome.

At the beginning of the toxic person encounter, what were both people like? Was one person strong and confident at the start of a relationship and now they appear weak and confused? Did one person seem to change over the course of the relationship to accommodate the needs or personality of the other person? Does it seem as if one person trained the other and now your friend or family member doesn't act like herself anymore? Is someone who used to be put together now falling apart? In *Man's Search For Meaning*, Victor Frankel said, *"An abnormal reaction to an abnormal situation is normal behavior."*

It is important to point out that after years of put downs from a toxic friend, coworker, or partner, the smart-girl/guy could suffer from low self-esteem, however; that does not mean that the relationship or situation began due to codependency issues or a lack of self-esteem. In fact, the presence of self-esteem issues after a toxic person encounter does not necessarily reflect the reason for the toxic person encounter. Toxic people are good at tricking and training! After having a toxic person encounter, it is easy to see that you (or someone else) ignored red flags at the early stages of the relationship or situation. However, a smart-girl/guy could have ignored those red flags because they believed in their ability to influence the situation—not because they needed to be needed or lacked self-confidence.

The first law of holes is well described by an adage that states: "If you find yourself in a hole, stop digging." Yet, smart-girl/guy syndrome says, "If you find yourself in a hole, dig harder and you can fix it." Soon, unfortunately, your arms are tired and you are covered in mud.

Smart-girls/guys aren't just good at working hard, they are often generous and kind as well. Giving people are good at giving. They don't want to create one-sided situations, so they don't assume that the other person in the relationship is trying to *create* a one-sided situation. While I absolutely agree that toxic relationships are one-sided, I believe that many smart girls or guys don't see that it's one-sided precisely because they aren't looking to get the better end of the deal. They are looking to do the right thing.

I firmly believe that we all see from our own perspectives. And, if you are a good, kind, loving, giving, and forgiving person, you assume that those in close proximity to you are also good, kind, loving, giving, and forgiving back. You assume that you are both trying to connect. You assume you are both working towards mutual goals. You assume you are both looking for win/win solutions. You assume you are both leading with the truth. You assume you are both willing to own your part in mistakes, and you assume you are both willing and able to work on or change deficits you bring to the relationship. If someone asked if you would be willing to sign up for a one-sided relationship, you would likely reply, "of course not!" Yet, how many of us have found ourselves in a one-sided relationship at some point in our lives?

The more invested you are in your relationships, the harder it may be to imagine that someone would purposely set you up to be in a one-sided situation. Yet, we cannot solve what we cannot see. The first step is recognizing that the relationship is one-sided. I believe this is easier said than done when you have been zipping along for years, assuming you are both doing the emotional work of the relationship. You feel like something is off and you know you are exhausted, but the toxic person keeps telling you that he or she is the only one doing the work within the relationship. You are confused, of course, so you keep working harder, yet it is never enough. You know you are exhausted, but you keep hoping that the next change you make will be the change that's needed to finally crack the code of never being good enough. Since you are the type of person who only gives criticism when it is needed, you assume a toxic person's criticisms are based in truth, and it's therefore your job to improve. You assume that when you improve yourself, the toxic situation will improve. Yet, it doesn't. Cycle, cycle, try, try, cry, cry, then try again. "Keep working! You are almost there!" you tell yourself. Yet, you never get there.

THE OTHER SIDE OF CODEPENDENCY

Codependency is also defined as a situation in which one person gets nearly all of their emotional needs met by another person. This is hardly ever the case in a toxic professional relationship, nor with a toxic friend, sibling, or toxic leader such as a pastor or priest. It's also rarely true of a romantic relationship in its earliest stages. Smart-girls/guys aren't looking for someone to meet all of their emotional needs; they are looking for companionship. However, after years together, they realize that, far too often, the toxic person has isolated them from outside sources of fulfillment and has become the sole voice in this person's life. At this point in the relationship, the smart-girl/guy is just trying to figure out a way to make life work so that their life doesn't fall apart.

Suggesting that a person is trying to get all their emotional needs met through another person does not tell the entire story. We are social creatures. We tend to do better when we have healthy relationships in our lives. People who have great friends report higher levels of happiness than people who do not have a tribe of friends they can trust. This is normal, not codependent. People who are happily married report higher rates of happiness than people who want to be married but have not yet found that right partner. That is normal, not codependent. People who have coworkers who care about them and a boss invested in their success report higher levels of happiness than people who are not connected to their work community. This is normal, not codependent.

We can all agree, I hope, that this way of relating to people is normal and healthy—until a toxic person enters the mix. It is at that point we start screaming about codependency. "What? Your husband/mother/daughter talked badly to you? Are you codependent? Why are you trying to get your emotional needs met through someone else? Do you have low self-esteem? Why are you so weak that you would put up with that? Can't you learn how to be alone?"

Notice in this scenario that the problem and focus become centered around blaming the person taking the brunt of the bad behavior rather than on the person exhibiting the bad behavior. In most circumstances, the person taking the brunt of the bad behavior isn't trying to get all of his or her needs met through another person. They are simply confused about the *behavior* of another person. And, at this point, they begin to become unsure about themselves.

After a toxic person encounter, it's hard to tell what the truth is. You know you have been running as hard as possible to make the other person in the relationship happy, but it feels like the finish line is always moving, and you are always losing. What do smart-girl/guys do when they start losing? They run faster, work harder, and refuse to quit!

HOW MUCH HELP IS TOO MUCH?

Codependency has also been also described as a relationship that enables another person to maintain his or her irresponsible, addictive, or underachieving behavior.[1] This is definitely true in many toxic person encounters, but the answer to the question "How much help is too much help?" is not clear in our society.

In one breath, parents are heralded for never giving up on their children, and in the next breath they are chastised for financially supporting their adult children. Is the parent who engages with a child in this way a codependent enabler, or selfless and supportive? In one breath, people celebrate the length of marriages through anniversaries, yet they don't take into account the quality of the marriage. The couple who fights like the mafia and hasn't touched each other in twenty years still gets a party and gifts because they stayed legally married for fifty years. Is this couple codependent? Or worthy of celebration?

How many chances does your sister deserve before you get called codependent? The answer to that question depends on who you ask. How many times does your boss get to yell at you before it is considered inappropriate? Again, the answer depends on who you ask. Are you a horrible person for putting your son out on the street, or are you a horrible person for not making him get a job? The answer depends on who you ask. What is the time limit before writing off your daughter due to her destructive life choices? Two months? Two years? Twenty years? Where is the handbook that defines how much is too much? At what point do you go from being caring to being codependent? Who gets to decide when enough is enough? Which is worse, giving up too easily or putting up with something for too long? You guessed it— it depends on who you ask and what *their definition* of codependency is.

Think about the years and years of practice you are expected to put in to become a world-class athlete, a remarkable violinist, an expert in your field, a high-quality consultant, a prominent speaker, or a leader in your marketplace. Achieving excellence takes time, patience, hard work, and dedication. Is it any wonder that people who have experienced success in other areas of life apply the same principles to their relationships? Is it really a surprise that they would rather put up with things a little too long (or a lot too long) and know they did everything they could rather than walk away too easily and too soon? Is it fair that this strength of character is used to hold them hostage in toxic situations? Is it fair to label them codependent when they try to get help?

SUMMARY

If you want to become Toxic Person Proof™, you have to start solving the right problems. If you are codependent, you should work with a codependency expert, read up on codependency, and develop a life outside of others. However, if you have smart-girl/guy syndrome, that is a completely different problem to solve.

To become Toxic Person Proof™, it's important to be aware that toxic people can (and will) use your strengths against you. Strengths such as your grit, your sheer desire to make things work, your belief that if something isn't working it means you need to work harder, your ability to hope, your belief in others, your loyalty, and your love.

Becoming clear about the true problem not only helps people move past the problem in a more significant way, it also prevents them from blaming others for the wrong problem. There is a difference between someone staying too long because they are a little too loyal and staying too long because they are a little too needy. There is a difference between someone giving a few too many chances and being a doormat. There is a difference between someone who believes in their ability to change (and therefore becomes willing to work harder to make something work) and someone who is just afraid of letting go. This approach is not only more honest in most circumstances, it is also more kind. People are more willing to get help when their intelligence, kindness, and loyalty have been used against them rather than trying to fix a codependency issue when they aren't codependent.

We learned from Cinderella's evil stepsisters that we shouldn't force on shoes that don't fit. We shouldn't force healing strategies that don't fit either. Give yourself the gift of 10 minutes and reflect on your experience with smart girl/guy syndrome so you can find the right healing strategy on your journey to become Toxic Person Proof™.

Chapter 7
I Need More Data

"Thinking too much leads to paralysis by analysis. It's important to think things through, but many use thinking as a means of avoiding action."

—Robert Herjavek

I will never forget a particular phone call.

As a toxic relationship specialist, I hear a *lot* of stories—a lot of stories that other people might deem crazy, while I just consider them part of a normal Thursday. People get on the phone with with me and say, "You won't believe what he or she did," and I reply with "I am one of the few people on earth who will not only believe what you tell me, but can probably *predict* what you will tell me." But, that particular night, I literally could not believe what I was hearing. And I was mad. Let me tell you a little about conversation I had with *Olivia. *Name has been changed to protect the absurdity.*

"Yeah, so I've been in a toxic relationship for a few years" Olivia started telling me. "He has been cheating on me, won't commit, tears me down, and makes me feel bad about myself. But I am doing really well."

"I'm glad to hear you are doing really well!" I replied. "So, I guess you have broken it off with him?"

"Well, no. I can't break it off with him because I am leading a class on narcissism." Olivia told me.

79

Confused about why leading a class on narcissism would make her reluctant to break up with her narcissistic partner, I said, "Wait, are you telling me that you are staying in a relationship with a narcissist so you can have more data for your class on narcissism?

"Yep," Olivia replied. "I really want to help other people. I figure, the more I know about narcissism in my life, the more information I will have to teach others."

I shifted uncomfortably in my seat and carefully asked, "Does that ever feel incongruent to you? That you would be trying to help other people *not* fall into narcissistic relationships while you yourself remain in a narcissistic relationship? Do you feel like something is off?"

"Not really. I mean, I'm sure the relationship will end." Olivia told me. "He is figuring some things out but will probably leave me for one of the other girls he is sleeping with."

"It seems like he is the one with all the choices in the relationship." I pointed out. "May I ask you something? If I told you I was teaching a class on snakes and was therefore putting myself into a pit of snakes and allowing myself to be bitten so I could have better knowledge for the class, what would you tell me?"

"Well, are the snakes poisonous?" Olivia asked.

My eyes got wide as I replied. "Do you think your relationship is poisonous?"

"No, not really." Olivia easily replied back.

"You told me that a committed, honest relationship where you are a priority was your number one goal. You are with someone who lies, tells you that you are worthless, and sticks his body part into other people's bodies. Do you not think this relationship is poisonous for you?" I asked worriedly

"Well, it is if you both agree that you are monogamous." Olivia told me.

Olivia and I went around this circle a few more times before ending the phone call. While I respect that we are all at our own stages of figuring ourselves out, I'm guessing that the people sitting in on her class on narcissism would not be thrilled to find out the information I did during our conversation. I doubt that her students would look kindly on the lack of boundaries in her life. This is the perfect example of the fact that knowing about toxic people and being Toxic Person Proof™ are not one and the same. Olivia was studying narcissism to avoid leaving someone she considered to be a narcissist. Studying him became her hobby, and she used "helping others" as an excuse to keep thinking about him. I felt sorry for the people in her class who were hoping to learn from her.

If you want to become Toxic Person Proof™, you do not need to know everything there is to know about toxic people. Forrest Gump taught us "life is like a box of chocolates—you never know what you are going to get." On the outside it may look like you are about to bite into chocolate and peanut butter goodness and instead end up with a mouth full of orange creme. It is nearly impossible to know what is inside a toxic person just by looking at their external shell. Toxic people come in an assortment of varieties, personalities, and professions. Just when you learn to protect yourself from one, you'll find yourself trying to figure out another personality type. It is much more effective to learn the various ways that you react when you are around toxic people and why you talk yourself out of seeing red flags. If you have had significant trauma or history with toxic people, you may need to work with a professional to reset how your body reacts to dangerous people and situations. If toxic behavior feels comfortable to you, you may miss these signals entirely, and further work will be needed.

THE DATA YOU DO NEED: LISTENING TO YOURSELF

"That's weird."

Memorize this phrase. Notice when people say it. Notice when you think it. Notice if it comes up when your partner is trying to tell you where he was last week. Notice if it comes up when someone is talking you into signing on the dotted line. Notice if it comes up with regard to so-called leaders. Notice if it comes up during a conversation with a friend.

In most circumstances, your body is smarter than your brain is. Your subconscious is likely to pick up on "that's weird" before you can readily identify exactly what is weird. I know we think we need the data to prove our suspicions. However, by the time you collect all the data, you will have already been sucked into the toxic situation. The feeling of "that's weird" *is the only data you need!* You don't need any more data than that in order to become Toxic Person Proof™. You need to simply start paying attention to the data your body is naturally picking up on.

I remember once when a dear friend introduced me to someone she intended to go into business with. I suggested to her that she not go through with it.

"Why?" She asked.

"I think something is off about her. I don't trust her. She didn't seem to react the way most people do." I answered. *Note: I had been friends with this person for several years, and we had built great trust in one another.*

"Do you know what you picked up on?" She asked curiously.

"I just don't trust her. And that's enough. You know how much I like people! So when I don't like someone, I take it as a seriously bad sign." I answered.

I understand why you want more data. But once you start to pay attention to the "that's weird" signals, you'll start to notice how often you are right. Sometimes, it takes years for all the data to come to light. If you set boundaries early on, those are years you will have spent protecting yourself from someone toxic. People often feel very nervous about doing this. They get caught up wondering, "*What* exactly is off? Do you think she is secretly embezzling money? Do you think he is a narcissist?"

By the time you fill in all the blanks and know all the reasons behind the odd feeling you have about someone, it will be too late. You will already be hurt. They will already have access to your business, your heart, or your children. By the time you fill in the blanks, you will already be emotionally engaged. You will already be unable to fully connect with your logic. Needing all the data *is* a blind spot. Act early!

TO BECOME TOXIC PERSON PROOF™, RECOGNIZE THAT NEEDING TO KNOW WHY IS A LIE.

"JUDGE ACTIONS, NOT INTENTIONS. Never try to 'mind-read' or second-guess why somebody is doing something, especially when they're doing something hurtful. There's no way for you to really know, and in the end, it's irrelevant. Getting caught up in what might be going on in an aggressor's mind is a good way to get side-tracked from the really pertinent issue. Judge the behavior itself. If what a person does is harmful in some way, pay attention to and deal with that issue."

—George K. Simon Jr., *In Sheep's Clothing: Understanding and Dealing With Manipulative People*

"IN ONE IMPORTANT WAY, an abusive man works like a magician: His tricks largely rely on getting you to look off in the wrong direction, distracting your attention so that you won't notice where the real action is. He draws you into focusing on the turbulent world of his feelings to keep your eyes turned away from the true cause of his abusiveness, which lies in how he thinks. He leads you into a convoluted maze, making your relationship with him a labyrinth of twists and turns. He wants you to puzzle over him, to try to figure him out, as though he were a wonderful but broken machine for which you need only to find and fix the malfunctioning parts to bring it roaring to its full potential. His desire, though he may not admit it even to himself, is that you wrack your brain in this way so that you won't notice the patterns and logic of his behavior, the consciousness behind the craziness."

—Lundy Bancroft, *Why Does He Do That? Inside the Minds of Angry and Controlling Men*

Fight the need to fill in the blanks. Teach your kids to fight it as well. More information on toxic personalities is not enough. We need to become Toxic Person Proof™.

Summary: We spend our time and energy focusing on and studying toxic people rather than protecting ourselves against toxic people. Our brains tell us that they are the same thing. They are not. To become Toxic Person Proof™, don't get sucked into the lie that you have to know why someone is behaving in a particular way. You do not need all the data to protect yourself. You just need to protect yourself. If something feels off or weird, there is usually something wrong. Pay attention if you feel a knot in your stomach or your face scrunches up as if you didn't understand something and needed clarification.

Take a few moments to reflect on the times when you suspected something might be wrong and you were right. Take inventory of the times in the past when you picked up on something being wrong. Strengthen this skill at every opportunity. Pay attention to the times when you pick up on something being weird, off, or wrong. Practice it first when you are not emotionally connected to the problem (remember the hot dog analogy), and then begin to incorporate it into situations to which you are emotionally connected. Figure out how your body tells you something is weird!

PART 2

STRATEGIES FOR DEALING WITH THE TOXIC PEOPLE IN YOUR LIFE

CHAPTER 8
THE KEY TO GETTING UNSTUCK

"We cannot solve our problems with the same thinking we used when we created them."

—Albert Einstein

One of the quickest ways to improve your life (especially after an encounter or relationship with a toxic person) is to learn to solve problems that have solutions. The key to getting unstuck is solving problems that have solutions rather than ruminating on problems that don't have solutions.

"But Sarah...I really want to have a different set of problems!"

"But Sarah...whyyyy do I have these problems?"

"But Sarah...if they changed, I wouldn't have any problems!"

"But Sarah...they have only been toxic for forty-four years. Surely, if I keep hoping, then they will be different when they are forty-five. I just need to keep thinking about it and hoping for it."

It's critical to note that there is a huge difference between changing toxic people and becoming Toxic Person Proof™. Have you ever heard the Serenity Prayer? *Grant me the serenity to accept the things I cannot change, the courage to change the things I can, and the wisdom to know the difference.* This prayer has stood the test of time for a reason and brought clarity to so many in so many situations.

Serenity comes from solving problems that have solutions. Courage doesn't require being courageous in solving *everyone's* problems; it requires courage in solving your own. It's about learning to be your own best problem solver and being wise enough to know which problems are actually yours to solve so that you can create a better life for yourself. I know you are probably hoping someone writes a book on how to change crocodiles into bunny rabbits. Yet despite TV dramas and storybook endings, when you look at real life, most people change by centimeters and inches rather than doing immediate 180-degree turns. The beast can learn better table manners, but beasts rarely turn into handsome princes. We *think they* turn into handsome princes, but in reality, they only wear the mask of a handsome prince while remaining true to their beastly insides. They simply learn to better cover up their bad behavior.

"But Sarah, don't you believe in people's ability to change?"

Yes, I do. But I also believe that there is a stack of data that says we want people to change more than *they* want to change. This leaves us beating our heads against the door of our own problems. If you want to become Toxic Person Proof™, you are going to need the wisdom to be able to see the difference between the people who really want to change and the people pretending to change in order to manipulate you. If you want to find true happiness, you need to solve a better set of problems rather than collide with the same problems over and over while wondering why you aren't getting different results.

Here is the world's simplest formula for creating a better life and becoming Toxic Person Proof™:

1. Recognize what the problem is.
2. Take action to solve the problem.

If you do this over and over and over again, you may not end up with a perfect life, but it's going to be pretty darn great. So often, however, we instead do the following:

1. Let a toxic person talk us into thinking we are the problem.
2. Ignore the problem because we don't want to believe the other person is toxic or is doing this on purpose. We pretend the problem isn't there, isn't that bad, or isn't going to affect our future.
3. Assume we have a communication problem rather than a toxic person problem.
4. Clump all our problems together so we don't know where to start, and then get overwhelmed and give up.
5. Ruminate over every aspect of the problem to avoid making changes or setting boundaries.
6. Talk ourselves into thinking we need to keep changing ourselves rather than realize we are losing a battle with a crocodile.
7. Find memes and social media posts that reinforce our belief that the problem will fix itself if we keep the faith.
8. Treat the crocodile bites rather than create a life wherein you aren't being bitten. Before long, crisis management, triage, and exhaustion become the new normal.
9. Rationalize the problem with thoughts like, "There must be a lesson to this." (Hint: the lesson is, learn to be a problem solver not a crocodile saver.)
10. Talk about the problem over and over (and over) again. In fact, we sometimes even pay people to listen to us talk about our problems over and over (and over).
11. Become a "help-aholic," worrying about everyone else's problems to avoid our own pain. We tell ourselves that we are being a good parent, a good friend, or a good community member, and we feel better for a while because it feels good to help people. But in the end, we always feel empty because we know we are secretly living a lie by giving advice we aren't willing to take ourselves.

My dad taught me from an early age that nothing ever changes without change. If you want to change your life, you have to *be* the change in your life. Period. The end. There isn't another way. That's it.

We will always have problems, and we are destined to live in a world where toxic people will always exist. However, if your life is a Groundhog Day of trying to solve toxic people problems over and over again, it is time to learn a new way of thinking so that you can become Toxic Person Proof™. If you continue to have the same problems again and again, it's a clear indicator that you are stuck. Don't allow yourself to get to the end of your life, reflect on who you have been, and realize you lived in a cycle of toxic relationships.

Other people aren't more lucky, more special, or more #Blessed than you. They simply figure out what problems they have in their lives, and they take action to solve them. Doing so isn't always cheap. It's almost never convenient. But it's *so* worth it. These individuals recognize toxic behaviors as toxic behaviors, and they design crocodile-free lives. A toxic-person-proof life is better (and *less* lonely, believe it or not) than one filled with toxic people. All experts agree on this fact because it's both simple and true. We are the ones who make it complicated because we don't want it to be true. Deep down, we want a different lesson to learn.

Learning to Break Down Problems: Spaghetti and Waffles

During the nine months I spent in my mother's belly, I estimate I consumed 1,459,302,576 pounds of tomatoes through my mother's diet. As a result, I've got a serious love relationship with pasta covered in red sauce. Lasagna is my first love language. Chicken parmesan makes me spontaneously combust into "Hallalujer," and ravioli have me salivating like a kid fondling a candy bar after returning home from fat camp. Of course, one cannot disregard the staple of the Italian diet: spaghetti. There is nothing better than poking that fork into a pile of saucy noodles and then letting the joy drip right down my throat.

But let's get real. Spaghetti is messy. Really messy. Proper single people know better than to order it on a first date, and proper social media posters know to take the pic in the white shirt *before* you dig into the dripping goodness. Have you ever tried to stab your fork into one noodle on a plate piled high with spaghetti? It's tough, right? The noodles are wound around one another, the sweet and savory sauce is holding the noodles together like glue, and the meatball is ready to roll off the plate without a moment's notice if you are not paying attention.

After a toxic person encounter, your thoughts are messy too. You often doubt reality, lack trust in yourself, and feel as if your problems are as interwoven as a big plate of spaghetti. You know there is a problem, but everything seems stuck together, and it is really difficult to differentiate one problem from the next. It is hard to fix one thing because you can't figure out what the one thing is that needs to be fixed. Or, as soon as you figure out that one thing, another problem pops up, then another, then another.

Toxic people are masters at getting you to focus on everything except the real problem: their behavior. They get you to focus on their feelings, their hurt, their past, their stress, and their sob story. Or they get you to focus on *you*—*your* past, your problems, your imperfections, and your insecurities. They are masters at making sure you can't pick up just one noodle because your state of confusion makes you easier to control.

The goal is to take your thought process from spaghetti to waffles. Waffles are easy to eat. Sure, with all the glorious butter and sugary syrup on top they can be a little messy, but life is a little messy and this is a metaphor, so go with me here. If I asked you to take a fork and cut out one waffle square, it would be pretty easy, right? Especially compared to trying to rescue one noodle from all its noodle brothers and sisters on the plate!

To become Toxic Person Proof™, you have to break your problems into boxes. Focus on one problem at a time, along with the art of redirecting your mind back to that one problem. Recognizing and protecting yourself against toxic behavior requires that you bite into that one problem at a time rather than try to solve a thousand problems all at once. It requires that you not allow your thoughts to flow like a river of sauce or allow yourself to become distracted by all the pieces of the past that are woven together like those spaghetti noodles I recently mentioned.

Here are some examples of getting clear around waffling down your problems into bite-sized pieces.

Spaghetti Problem: I might need to change jobs. My coworker is making me miserable, but if I leave I am going to have to tell my wife, and she is going to be mad, and I am afraid I won't be able to pay for my daughter's college. *It is nearly impossible to figure out what problem you need to solve in this scenario.*

Waffle Problem: How am I going to respond the next time my coworker says something about me that isn't true? *Is this your problem to solve? Yes! Do you have control of the outcome of the problem? Yes! Can you take action on this problem and make your life better? Yes!*

Spaghetti Problem: I'm getting upset just thinking about being around my aunt at the reunion. She always makes me feel like such a failure. I don't even want to go this year, but if I don't go, my mom will make me feel like a horrible daughter, and then I will have to figure out how to make it up to her. *It is nearly impossible to figure out what problem you need to solve in this scenario.*

Waffle Problem: How can I avoid being alone with my aunt at the family reunion? If I find myself alone with her, what will I do/say to put more physical distance between us? *Is this your problem to solve? Yes! Do you have control of the outcome of the problem? Yes! Can you take action on this problem and make your life better? Yes!*

We all have complicated problems in our lives, but we can't solve any problem in our lives if we don't learn how to become better problem solvers. Solving simpler problems through action builds momentum and helps us get unstuck! It also helps us become better problem solvers when we are faced with our biggest challenges. After a toxic person encounter, you may feel helpless and insecure in your ability to solve problems. Use the exercise below to build up your confidence and take back your life!

Summary: Becoming Toxic Person Proof™ involves learning what problem you are trying to solve, figuring out if it is a problem that can be solved (something in your control), and then taking action on that problem. When you get overwhelmed, try to waffle down the problem into one specific bite. Try not to get sucked into being distracted by interweaving all the problems together so that they feel overwhelming. Give yourself the gift of 10 minutes and work through the problem-solving exercise below.

1. What problem am I trying to solve?

2. Am I responsible for this problem or am I trying to solve someone else's problem for them? (If it is not your problem to solve, find a different problem.)

3. Is solving this problem something that I can control? Does this problem have a solution that I can influence? (If it is not something you can control, find a different problem.)

4. What very specific problem am I looking to solve? Can I break down the problem into smaller components? (And then, can you break it down even more?)

5. Am I trying to solve a problem or not feel an emotion? If I am feeling a difficult emotion, how can I separate my emotions and tap into logic as I try to figure out what problem to solve? (If you are having trouble separating your emotions from your problems, get two pieces of paper and write your emotions on one page and your problems on the other.)

6. What are three action steps I can take toward solving the problem?

CHAPTER 9
MENTAL STRATEGIES TO EMPLOY WHEN YOU CAN'T JUST WALK AWAY

"This is a society that thinks every problem has a solution."
—Esther Perel

How much easier would life be if there were an easy solution for dealing with toxic people, or if they wanted to change and follow the rules of society? How nice would it be if we didn't have to worry about this stuff? Novelist Taylor Jenkind Reid described "a world that is moral and just where the good guys win and the bad guys lose, where the pain you face is only in an effort to make you stronger so that you can win much bigger in the end." How lovely would it be to live in a world that makes sense? A world in which every problem has a solution. A world in which it's easy to spot the bad guys and our superheroes, and fairy godmothers will come to our rescue if things get too tough. A world where our struggles make us stronger so that we win much bigger in the end.

Put simply, sometimes the world is not moral. Sometimes the bad guys win, and we are left to clean up their messes and put our hearts back together. "It isn't fair!" we scream internally, as we fight for a solution that makes sense. Sometimes people don't change. Sometimes families and businesses break up. Sometimes life doesn't fit into convenient boxes.

So, what do we do when we can't just walk away from toxic people?

I have been fortunate enough to have the opportunity to talk to a multitude of experts on toxic people and toxic situations. They agree on the following:

1. Toxic people exist.
2. Toxic people hurt your life.
3. Toxic people (and people in general) aren't going to change unless they decide to change.
4. Your energy is best spent trying to change anything other than them.
5. The fewer toxic people you have in your life, the better.

The experts agree that the more toxic people you have in your life, the more likely you will be to experience frustration, confusion, health issues, and unhappiness. Yet, a world with no toxic people isn't our reality. That being said, please don't use this chapter as a loophole for putting up with bad behavior. I hear the term "staying well," but I hardly ever see anyone actually "staying well." I see them numbing, medicating, self-medicating, and dying emotionally before they actually die physically.

The solution to handling toxic people is not becoming an expert at putting up with toxic behavior.

You can control who you are around, but you can't control who others are around, and their choices affect your life as well. Think about the woman you love being used by her adult child. Think about the man you love being beaten down by his boss. Think about the friend you respect going back to the partner who doesn't respect her. Think about loving your children, and not loving the person with whom you had the children. These aren't people who you can pretend don't exist. There is not a toxic people island to which we can send people. There are wonderful people who are in relationships with toxic adult children, toxic business partners, or toxic friends. There are wonderful situations that are perfect—except for this one thing. There are wonderful lives that are great—except for this one thing. There are wonderful careers that only require managing that jerk from marketing a couple times a year. There are wonderful families that only require dealing with the sketchy uncle a few times a year. This chapter details how to manage those situations.

All that said, I want you to think of these solutions as pain medication rather than a cure. At the time I am writing this, I have an aunt who is battling cancer. I want a cure to be discovered for her, however I also want to give her pain medication. The pain meds are not going to cure her cancer, but they can make her pain more bearable and manageable. Creating distance between you and toxic people is a bit like curing cancer. The following strategies are like the pain meds you use when you can't avoid toxic people entirely. They are certainly not meant to cure toxic people, however they can help make your life more bearable when you have no other choice but to deal with them.

GET YOUR MIND CLEAR: SURVIVAL STRATEGIES

The best way to survive toxic person encounters is to lower your expectations. A toxic person isn't likely to apologize or admit to being wrong or see the light! You cannot outsmart a toxic person into developing a different personality. You can't force them to be different. Therefore, it is helpful to change your mindset and think about surviving toxic situations and thriving in non-toxic situations. If you try to thrive within toxic situations, you are going to be extremely frustrated. Your goal is simply *to survive*, not to change the toxic person.

One of the best ways to lower your expectations is to recognize the difference between a problem to solve and a crisis to manage.

Problem to Solve: A situation where we have control of the outcome. We can get clarity and take action, and things will likely be different after we take that action. We may not like the prob-lem we are faced with, however we can influence the outcome in a significant way.

Crisis to Manage: Managing a crisis is like saving a burning house by figuring out which part of the fire to put out first. When you have a crisis to manage, you are grappling with multiple things you can't control—things that are not about you at all.

For example, John has lost three jobs in the last year. His inability to work is a crisis to manage, not a problem that you can solve. Only John can solve the problem that exists. Annie continues to struggle with her addiction and refuses to get help. Her addiction and its effects on others is a crisis to manage, not a problem to solve. Devin is a nineteen-year-old who keeps getting in trouble with authority. He is technically an adult, and keeps having run-ins with the law. He refuses help. Creating or kicking him out if he doesn't get that help is a problem you could solve, but otherwise the situation is a crisis to manage.

Toxic people cause crises. We are wasting our time when we approach those crises as problems we can solve. We need to lower our expectations with regard to how much influence we have on the situation. There are always things in our life that we can't control, yet they greatly affect us—things like pandemics, severe illness, war, death, and trying to save toxic people from their latest tragedy. These are things you can't really get good at. Frankly, these are things it would be crazy to try to get good at! These are things you are forced to *work around*, not things that you can solve.

Surviving life with toxic people means that you have a crisis to manage, not a problem to solve. For people to change, they have to *want to* solve their own problems. By definition, toxic people do not want to take responsibility for or solve their own problems. They want you to do the work for them.

STOP THINKING SOMEONE IS GOING TO BE BETTER

For the record, lowering your expectations also requires that you stop being surprised when someone acts like him- or herself.

Stop being surprised when the alcoholic shows up drunk, even if it is Grandma's 80th birthday. Stop being surprised when your mother-in-law criticizes your life choices with every chance she gets. Stop being surprised when the guy who constantly ghosts you disappears when a new piece of hot flesh comes along. Stop being surprised when your irresponsible spouse quits yet another job because he is so stressed out. Stop being surprised when your friend calls needing you to save her from her newest tragedy. Stop being surprised when your adult child quits his job because he knows you are going to keep bailing him out. Stop being surprised when your ex refuses to be flexible about the parenting decisions. Stop being surprised when your jealous husband gets mad and sabotages the evening right before you are eligible for a promotion. Yes, they know what they are doing. No, they don't want to change. Why? Because they like living this way—it allows them to get what they want more than it allows you to get what you want. In fact, when asked to change their behavior, toxic people typically change the people they are around rather than changing who they are. Typically, they would rather change their surroundings than change their behavior. This allows them to avoid responsibility.

When people act out of character, *then* get surprised. When people act like themselves, however, please stop acting surprised.

"Gosh, you won't believe what she is doing now!"

"I just can't believe that out of all the days, he would make things about him today."

"I just can't believe someone would act like this."

"I just can't believe she hasn't grown up a little bit."

"I can't believe he would act like that in front of our boss."

"I can't believe she hasn't gotten herself together by now."

"I can't believe he can't work with me in the best interests of the rest of the family."

Believe it! Stop being surprised! Accept it! Yes, your life would be better if they behaved better. You have tried to help. You have tried to communicate differently. You have hoped and forgiven and been patient and given one hundred second chances. Did it work? Probably not. Because this is who they choose to be. This is who they *want* to be. This is how life works best for them. The promises to change were promises made simply to get you off their back and manage their image. If they truly wanted to be better, they would get their own help rather than consistently having you be the only one trying to provide the help. Stop being surprised that they keep being who they are.

I know these mindset shifts aren't what you want when you can't just walk away, however this particular mindset shift is huge because it **helps you save your energy for problems that actually have solutions.** Toxic situations are best handled with your best self. Your most rested self. You least confused self. Your realistic self. When you keep being surprised when someone acts like themselves, it sends your brain into confusion. Confusion makes you tired. Being tired means that you don't bring your best self to the situation, and not bringing your smartest brightest self to the situation creates a situation in which you aren't as likely to see toxic behavior and handle it well.

Have you ever heard someone say, "I was at the end of my rope"? No one lives their best life at the end of their rope. You need energy in order *not* to reach the end of your rope. Don't use your energy being surprised when they act like themselves. Use your energy to protect yourself rather than to figure them out. You have already figured them out—you just don't like what you figured out!

Confusing a problem to solve (your next career, where you are going on vacation, fixing the flat tire) with a crisis to manage (their personality) is like ramming your head into a door hoping that they will eventually open the door. If it doesn't work, stop doing it. What does the pattern of behavior tell you about who they are? Believe the data. You aren't a bad person for stepping away from the door and grabbing some headache medication. Find things you can do to make your life better. Find problems that have solutions. Find better problems to solve. Find better things to talk about.

FIND A NEW HOBBY

"Sarah, are you suggesting that I NEVER talk about my toxic people problem with others? Shouldn't I get an outside perspective and gain wisdom for others and not try to do life alone? Isn't talking this out a healthy coping mechanism?"

Many of us need to debrief a situation in order to get clarity about it. Many of us need to talk it out to work it out. Holla to all my fellow extroverts! I am not talking about ignoring what is happening, stuffing it down, or pretending it doesn't exist. But I am talking about finding a new hobby. **Too many people's hobbies consist of talking about toxic people doing the same things over and over and over.** Imagine an alien flying down from space one year and hearing you say, "I can't believe they did that" and then watching them flying down from space two years (or twenty years) later and listening in to another one of your conversations and hearing you say the same thing: "I can't believe they are still doing that?"

Now, I don't necessarily believe in aliens, but I do believe that aliens would not think much of human intelligence if they peeked into many of our conversations on toxic people. My guess is that the alien would say, "Why do these humans not get it? If you put your hand in hot water, you'll get burned every time. Why do these humans think the water will not be hot this time? Why do they not learn? Why do they hope the water will be different next time if only they wish for it badly enough? Why do they keep talking about the same thing over and over, and expecting there to be different results?"

I understand how maddening it is and that venting with others and ruminating can trick you into feeling like you are solving a problem. Discussing ways you wish another person would change can feel like problem solving, but if it is a crisis to manage, there is no problem to solve. If you are working with an expert who understands toxic behaviors, you will be able to find problems you can solve *within* the crises you have to manage. Most of your friends and family are unable to help you in this way, and will instead probably give you bad advice. Every lunch you spend venting to your girlfriends raises your blood pressure. Every time you go home to complain to your wife, you bring the anger of work into the peace of home. If you are like me and need to say it out loud to get it out of your head, okay! But make it short and sweet. Don't let it take over the entire night or the entire conversation.

Stop using phrases such as "I can't believe they are acting like this." Tell your brain you *can* believe it and you *should* believe it because they have been acting like this for the last five years. Save the "I can't believe it!" for the moment when they improve their behavior and demeanor. Remind yourself that they are being exactly who they are. In fact, they are being exactly who they want to be because their choices are getting them exactly what they want. We all can make the choice to change lifestyles that don't work for us. Toxic people's actions have shown very clearly that they don't have a problem with their lifestyle, while you *do* have a problem with *their* lifestyle. Stop being surprised by what you already know to be true.

Stop hoping they will get better and start making your life better. Stop being surprised when they act like themselves. Save your effort and energy for something that is going to get you results.

LAST BUT NOT LEAST, THE EMOTIONAL CUSHION

Throughout time, we have been wrong about many, many things. We used to think the earth was flat. We used to think evil spirits lived in brussels sprouts. We used to think men who suffered from erectile dysfunction could be cured by goat testicle implants. This is true; look it up. This is also helpful to point out because the man claiming he was able to provide resurrections, I mean erections, was not, in fact, a doctor. He just told people he was a doctor and they let him cut his way right in. He later ran for governor of Kansas after making millions through his false promises. So, if you ever feel stupid after being duped by a toxic person, just repeat these two little words: goat gonads. You will instantly feel better. At least you didn't get duped into getting goat gonads. I'm thinking of getting the words "Goat Gonads" printed on a t-shirt to remind myself and others. It's a great conversation starter—if you have trouble starting conversations.

Another thing we got wrong was telling ourselves that the purpose of boundaries was to change the other person. Remember, "Better boundaries don't make better wolves." So often when we set boundaries, go no contact, or make long-term changes to the relationship, we think it will change the behavior of the toxic person. We think that if we have the hard talk, our family members will behave. We think that if we get the divorce, we can stop the fighting. We think that if we work from home to avoid the jerk in the next cubicle, we won't have to deal with jerks. We think that if we can get the right kind of healing, we can stop attracting toxic people. We are wrong.

Setting boundaries, filling our lives with people who treat us well, and creating distance with people who have a pattern (remember the pattern!) of not treating us well is a lifelong journey. Many of us are also in situations where dealing with toxic people in some form or fashion is also a lifelong journey. If your brain is saying, "Oh, well then there is no reason to do the work of cutting the toxic person out of my life," I want to remind you that life can get better. It can get *so* much better. You can't make the crocodile turn into a bunny, and you can't make crocodiles not exist. But you *can* stop wrestling with a crocodile every day. Life is significantly better when you are not wrestling with a crocodile every day.

It is important to acknowledge that just because the status of the relationship changes, that does not mean the toxic person will change. It just means that you will give them less opportunity to hurt you. It means you are putting more space and protection between you and the toxic person.

Our lives are like swimming pools. Toxic people are like the jerks that pee in the pool. Their poison spreads to everyone in the pool. We can move to the other end of the pool and add more chlorine, but it doesn't make them stop peeing. However, if you are dealing with them every day, it isn't like being in a pool with them. It is like drinking their poison (dare I say pee) from a cup. It's a nasty visual, I know, but we are talking about toxic people, so sometimes we need nasty reminders to keep ourselves safe. Would you rather swim in pee or drink it? Easy decision, right?

Even after changing the status of the relationship and enforcing boundaries, we still need to figure out ways to keep our lives as clean and urine-free as possible. Yes, I realize life would be easier if toxic people would just go away. Yes, I realize life would be easier if toxic people found someone else's pool to pee in. Yes, I realize toxic people should act better, and this isn't fair. I really, really do. But let's focus on the problems we actually have rather than the problems we wish we had. Let's keep you safe, shall we? I promise, it will be less painful than having goat balls stapled to your most private parts.

If you have a significant toxic person in your life who you still interact with, it can be really helpful to think of it as a disease. On my dad's side of the family, there are so many family members who have diabetes. I remember being at my grandmother's house, opening the fridge, and seeing insulin ready to administer when needed. She always had orange juice and candy bars at the ready in case her blood sugar dropped. She had a calendar marked with doctor appointments and a bowl on the kitchen counter that housed her medications. She could have pretended she didn't have diabetes. She could have been angry about the diabetes and talked about diabetes with all her girlfriends. Or, she could have prepared for diabetes and moved on with her life.

If you have to deal with a toxic person and try to be happy while doing so, think of preparing for your encounter with the toxic person like you would prepare for having a disease. You have to stop pretending the toxic person isn't there and prepare accordingly. Can you imagine me calling my grandmother and having the following exchange:

Nana: "You won't believe it! I had to drink orange juice because my blood sugar dropped!"

Me: "Well, yeah Nana, you have diabetes."

Nana: "What? I shouldn't have diabetes. I can't believe diabetes acted like that. I can't believe diabetes made my insulin drop. I can't believe diabetes is doing that to me!"

If this were what my Nana was saying, we would be worried about more than just her blood sugar!

Now let's go to the conversations most people have about toxic people.

Them: "You won't believe it! I had to change my entire schedule because of a toxic person!"

Me: "Well, sounds like you have a toxic person for sure. They are pretty selfish."

Them: "What I shouldn't have to change my schedule. I can't believe the toxic person acted like that. I can't believe the toxic person made me change my schedule. I can't believe the toxic person is acting like this again!"

In a perfect world, my grandmother doesn't die of diabetes. In a perfect world, people act in the best interests of those around them. But if someone has a pattern of doing the wrong thing, it is helpful to prepare ahead of time. Nana had medicine. Appointments. Chocolate in her purse. You need back-up plans. Information on how to protect yourself. Mental health appointments. Chocolate in your purse.

We spend too much time being surprised by toxic people's behavior rather than planning for toxic people to act like toxic people. "You are not going to believe what they did!" and "I just can't believe they keep acting like this" and "I thought that once I set boundaries, things would be different!" is like Nana thinking her blood sugar wasn't ever going to drop. Diabetes has a pattern. Toxic people have a pattern. Sometimes the pattern is predictably unpredictable, but it is still a pattern. And the pattern is working in their favor rather than working in your favor.

Plan for toxic people to continue pulling the same stuff. If someone were going to the doctor surprised that she had diabetes, we would help them move into acceptance. If we keep being surprised that toxic people act toxic, we need to gently move into acceptance. Diabetes sucks. It shapes your life, and you have to do things differently than you would if you didn't have that disease. Toxic people suck. Having them in your life shapes your life, and you have to do things differently than you would if you didn't have them in your life.

Internationally renowned parental alienation coach Amy J.L. Baker told me in an interview we had together that most people can be pretty good parents after a divorce and things will be fine. However, if you are dealing with someone who is trying to turn your kids against you, you have to be an A++ parent to keep a healthy relationship with your kids. She also says that if your co-parent is trying to turn your kids against you, there may have been very little you could have done differently. Please do not read that statement and hear me saying that you were not a good parent if a toxic person poisoned your kids against you. That was not the point of this example. The point of the example is that we have to do things differently if we have a toxic person in our lives. Is it fair? No. But if you have a disease or a toxic person, you have to do things differently than you would if you didn't. Simply pretending you don't have to prepare for a disease or a toxic person is a bad strategy.

If you had diabetes, you would check in on yourself daily to make sure your insulin was at the proper level. You would have both crisis management solutions (such as a piece of candy) and long-term solutions (like daily medication) to avoid crisis. Thinking of the stress and turmoil caused by a toxic person the same way you'd think about the stress and turmoil caused by not properly managing diabetes. You need to check on your emotional health daily, practice stress reducing activities, and keep checking in with yourself to ensure that you do not get to the end of your rope. Getting to the end of your rope could result in an unfortunate blow up at work or an unfortunate blow up in front of your kids. Both are no-nos.

Where a toxic person situation is concerned, it is important to have both crisis management solutions and long-term solutions close at hand. Crisis management solutions could include knowing ahead of time what will you say if someone throws you under the bus in a meeting or at a family dinner. Crisis management could also include coming up with backup plans if someone falls through on promises such as having a work assignment completed or picking up the kids from school. Long-term solutions could include planning to move to a different team at work, getting a divorce, or creating a tribe of friends so you don't have to spend as much time with your toxic family or family member.

If you have a toxic person in your life, you need to make life choices that allow you to have an emotional cushion around yourself to protect yourself from the toxic person in the same way that a diabetic would need to pack insulin to protect herself from a drop in blood sugar. Have you ever seen those inflatable plastic balls that humans can fit inside and use to roll down a mountain? I want you to imagine having that same kind of ball (but invisible) all around you as an emotional cushion. Everywhere you go, you are protected from every angle from everything on the outside. The emotional cushion protects you so that when a toxic person pokes and prods you like a maniacal rancher trying to brand a calf, you have an emotional cushion around you to protect yourself.

TRADITIONAL SELF-CARE VS AN EMOTIONAL CUSHION

The world of makeup, spas, and shopping has taken over self-care, and many of us have it built into our heads that self-care is selfish. If you're in that camp, drop the world self-care and take up the phrase "I need to build my emotional cushion." See what changes for you. A good night's sleep builds your emotional cushion. Saying no when you are already too busy protects your emotional cushion. Not spending too much time around people who drain you protects your emotional cushion. Spending time on hobbies and interests you love builds your emotional cushion. When you are tired, stressed, and at the end of your rope, you have no emotional cushion available, and a toxic person encounter can push you right over the edge. When you are rested, happy, healthy, and full of life, the same toxic person encounter doesn't have nearly the same negative impact on you.

An emotional cushion also protects your healthy relationships. Few (if any) adults speak about their childhood by saying, "My parents were so well rested, well balanced, full of life, and genuinely at peace with themselves. They took care of themselves in a way that allowed them to raise me with patience, love, and an appropriate tone of voice. They refused to keep me in bad situations and led by example in having healthy boundaries. I had a really horrible upbringing." No boss says, "That person is just so emotionally healthy. She really brings down the company." No worthy date says, "I feel like she is self-reflective and has really broken free of her past baggage. No way is she a good catch." Emotional cushions...just get one. Everyone in your life will be better for it! Especially you!

Summary: When you are going to be around a toxic person, it is important to have mental strategies in place to protect you mentally and emotionally. Give yourself the gift of 10 minutes and list out some ways you can build an emotional cushion around yourself to protect yourself. What is a phrase you need to stop using? Do you need to lower your expectations? What boundaries do you need to give yourself around talking about your toxic person? What are some mental strategies you can use to increase your energy level?

CHAPTER 10
COMMUNICATING WITH TOXIC PEOPLE

"Wise men speak because they have something to say;
Fools because they have to say something."

—Plato

If you have tried to use reason and logic to talk to a toxic person,
you probably already know that typical communication skills do
not work. A toxic person's goal is not to fix a problem. A toxic
person's goal is to make you feel like *you* are the problem. Some
toxic people literally get a high from controlling you and watching
you squirm. Some just want to avoid responsibility and keep up
their image, so anything you say will be held against you. Some
just want to have their way and truly don't care what you say at all.

Communicating with this type of person feels much like the old
phrase "You are the rubber I am the glue. Whatever you say bounces
off me and sticks to you." Prepare to be frustrated, and don't be
surprised when they spew blame. I've seen countless people try to
extend olive branches of peace, only to have the toxic person turn
around and hit them with their own branch. Far too often, if you
try to appeal to their kindness, they will say you are manipulative.
If you try to stand strong, they will say you are controlling. And,
if you don't communicate at all, they will say you are negligent.

I am getting mad even typing these words. I get it. It isn't fair. They should be better. It shouldn't be this hard. But...it is. We must solve the problems we have rather than the problems we wish we had. You can either get mad that there is a problem, or you can try to solve the problem. If there is a toxic person you can't get away from, you are going to have to learn how to communicate with him or her. Here are several ways to get your point across without losing your mind:

1. TOXIC PEOPLE DON'T HAVE EARS WILLING TO HEAR

When you are trying to get your point across to others, the first thing you need to ask yourself is "Do they have ears willing to hear? Is there any way I can get through to them in this situation, or have they already decided?" You can be the best communicator in the world, but you cannot teach others to grow ears that are willing to actually hear. If someone has *already decided* that you are responsible for every problem in their life and in the relationship, your words are not the issue. The issue is that they don't have ears willing to hear. If someone is determined to avoid getting into trouble and you come in with a stack of data proving your point, your data isn't the problem; the problem is they don't have ears willing to hear. If you are trying to talk an accomplice into seeing the truth about their partner in crime, it doesn't matter what you say. That person doesn't have ears willing to hear.

Talking to someone who refuses to see the truth into trying to see the truth is difficult because that person doesn't have ears willing to hear. Why? Because they aren't looking for the whole truth; they are merely looking for the truth that is most convenient for them. You are not engaging in a normal conversation. Toxic people are not interested in a win/win situation based on mutual interests. They are out to make you feel like a loser so that they can feel like a winner or offload responsibility for the situation. Appealing to logic or listing out the true facts will likely leave you feeling extremely frustrated if they do not have ears willing to hear you.

I will never forget the advice a family therapist gave to me. He said, "You keep making logical arguments for an emotional problem." I was so frustrated when I heard those words, but I knew he was right. Thanks, Tim! Oftentimes, the problem isn't the logic. Or the data. Or the choice of words. The toxic person has an agenda of protecting their ego, reputation, or denial, and if your words do not fit in with their perspective of the world, they refuse to grow ears willing to hear.

If someone has ears willing to hear, logic, data points, and clear communication are the approaches that will be successful. If someone has an emotional block, recognize that logic and data points will not work if they have already decided what they want to believe. Saying more words is not likely to help. The problem is that you are talking to the wrong type of ears. someone has decided they do not want to see the truth about a situation, they will shut off their ears when you come in with data.

Let's look at an example that will make it easy to see how this plays out in a scenario we can all likely identify with. Imagine that young Adam has been acting up in school, and so his parents have to go in for a parent-teacher conference. The teacher is distraught over how badly Adam has been behaving, and she is hoping to get support from his parents. She carefully crafts the conversation in her head. She brings copies of male anatomy he has drawn on other students' math papers. She also brings a short story wherein he outlines the delights of his playground antics where he gives the other boys purple yurples (look it up) and teaches the little girls dirty words.

Adam's parents do not have ears willing to hear, so they blame the teacher, the video games, and the bad kids he has been spending time with—without any acknowledgment that he is the biggest troublemaker in the class, by far. Is the problem a lack of data on the teacher's end? Is the problem the fact that her collegiate experience did not give her more or better tools for communication? Or, is the problem that the parents have an emotional resistance to seeing their son as the problem because, if they did, they would have to take a deeper look at their parenting practices? In their minds, if another child were calling kids names and ruining their schoolwork, it would be a problem. In fact, the parents would readily agree that these behaviors were not acceptable. They just can't believe *their* child is behaving unacceptably, so they minimize the significance of the behaviors as soon as the behavior is applied to their child.

Now, imagine what happens when Adam grows up. He has avoided taking responsibility for his behavior since he was a young child and has no interest in starting now. Adam has become skilled at avoiding responsibility through manipulation tactics and is used to winning arguments by blaming his behavior on anyone and everyone else. His parents were good at this, and later in life Adam will be great at it as well.

Adam's boss might want to talk to him about a complaint he received from a customer who said that Adam was rude to him on the phone. The boss will try to use logic and data to talk Adam into speaking differently to the customer, but will leave the conversation thinking the customer was actually the problem because of Adam's skillful blame shifting. The boss will be a little confused and not sure what really happened. The boss will then ask himself, "Should I have said something differently? Did the customer say something I missed?"

Adam's wife will likely also be questioning herself and trying to perfect her own communication styles. She will have tried a thousand different ways of convincing Adam to be a more active participant in his daughter's life. Adam will flip the conversation and say his wife is trying to offload even more responsibility on him, and she should be grateful that he works and she gets to sit home all day. His wife will be baffled. She works from home, but actually has more career responsibilities than Adam does. She will try to use logic to point out her career and household responsibilities. Will Adam care? Will he have ears willing to hear her very true logic? Her facts? The data? Will she need to bring in a spreadsheet? No. And, it won't be because she did a poor job of making a solid case. It will be because her husband does not have ears willing to hear. The issue was never the words of the teacher, the boss, or the wife. The issue was that Adam didn't have ears willing to hear.

Recognize when you are talking to someone who has an agenda for not hearing you, not believing you, not listening to you, or not communicating with you. If they don't have ears willing to hear because they don't *want* to hear, don't waste your time and energy beating yourself up over your inability to communicate. Your words aren't the problem. You are going to have to employ a different strategy than simply choosing clearer words.

2. WHAT DO YOU WANT? WHAT DO THEY WANT?

Everybody wants something. Be aware that not everyone you communicate with is looking for a mutual solution. Do they want to protect their image? Protect their money? Avoid responsibility? Fight so they are the center of your attention? Before the discussion, figure out what you want, and figure out what you are willing to give up in order to get what you want.

Examples of "bad" things to want:

1. I want you to apologize.
2. I want you to see how badly you hurt me.
3. I want you to see how destructive your behavior is.
4. I want to prove you were wrong so that you'll give me credit for being right.
5. I want you to see how hard I have been working to get this relationship to work.
6. I want you to see how mean/selfish/unfair you are being.
7. I want you to do the right thing.
8. I want you to do what is best for others.
9. I want you to be a team player.

Instead of trying to communicate these things, just get one of those ninja boards you see on karate videos and practice ramming your head through it. I've never broken a board with my head, but if the internet videos are legitimate, it seems to work sometimes. Working sometimes is better than working never.

Trying to get toxic people to make changes from the above list will never work. They will be happy to *tell you* they will change these things so they can trick you, but it will definitely go on the NEVER list rather than the SOMETIMES list. Don't believe me? Make a timeline of all the times a toxic person promised he or she was going to do better and ended up right back at the place of being themselves again.

Examples of "good" things to want:

1. I want you to take the kids to baseball on Thursday.
2. I want to have Christmas dinner at your house.
3. I want to come up with a schedule for the project.
4. I want the budget sheet you promised me a week ago.
5. I want the credit card statement.
6. I want to know when the doctor's appointment is.
7. I want you to be home at 11:00 (example for teens).

Do you see how these requests have clear objectives rather than asking the other person to act differently? Be crystal clear about your objective and what you want. Do NOT go into a conversation with a toxic person without knowing what you want or having some plan around what you want. Do NOT go in thinking you will figure out what you want together, because if you do, the toxic person will always get what *they* want while you walk away wondering what happened. They are going to find a way to flip it back on you somehow. Be prepared and stick to the topic at hand.

Is it fair to ask a parent or partner or coworker to be better, take responsibility, and work on the relationship? Absolutely, 100 percent, yes. Yet, if you have been trying to be better, change yourself, and communicate differently without seeing any change from the toxic person, it's a good time to switch to this strategy. Remember, this is a survival strategy after nothing else works, not a message that we should all become heartless robots. If someone wants to avoid working with you or giving you what you want, they are going to try to get you off topic as quickly as possible. They will make you feel badly for asking what you want.

Here are some ways a toxic person could manipulate you into changing topics, and ways to get them back on track in a respectful manner:

1. I want you to take the kids to baseball on Thursday.

    - Them: What kind of parent doesn't want to spend time with their kids? Why don't you want to take them? Are you not focused on being a good father/mother?
    - You: Are you going to be able to take them on Thursday, or do I need to make other arrangements?

2. I want to have Christmas dinner at your house.

    - Them: What kind of daughter are you? We do it at your house every year, and our mother is getting older by the day. I can't believe you are being so selfish and breaking tradition.
    - You: My house is not an option this year. Will your house be available?

3. I want to come up with a schedule for the project.

    - Them: Gosh, I have just been so busy and then this happened and then this happened and then this happened, etc. Or, What? No one told me I was in charge of that? Why didn't Amy handle it?
    - You: What is your timeline for getting that turned in? I need it by Wednesday at the latest.

4. I want the budget sheet you promised me a week ago.

    - Them: I am the only one in this office who turns anything in on time, and yet you are always on my back. Why don't you ever come down this hard on anyone else?
    - You: When will I have the budget sheet on my desk?

5. I want the credit card statement.

    - Them: Don't you trust me? You have some serious
      issues going on that you need to work through if you
      can't trust your own spouse. Plus, I have been super
      busy taking care of everything. Maybe if you would
      step up your game around here, I would have more
      time to do you favors.
    - You: Is the credit card statement available here at the
      house, or should I contact the credit card company?

6. I want to know when the doctor's appointment is.

    - Them: You have to control everything. You are such a
      control freak.
    - You: Can you give me a time, or should I contact the
      office myself?

Notice how the suggested responses bring the conversation
right back on topic? The suggested responses are not mean. They
don't blame, name call, or create more drama. In actuality, they
are kind of boring. If they lead you into blaming or defending
yourself, you will not get what you want from the conversation.
Stay on topic with regard to what you want when a toxic person
tries to get you off topic by shifting the focus or trying to make
you feel bad. Here are some examples of how you could approach
the conversation that would *not* allow you to win the conversation
and would instead ensure that you both get off point:

1. I want you to take the kids to baseball on Thursday.

    - Them: What kind of parent doesn't want to spend time
      with their kids? Why don't you want to take them? Are
      you not focused on being a good father/mother?

- You: Are you freaking kidding? I am always at the house taking care of things and you are always off doing whatever you want. They kids would be lost without me.
- You: Why would you say I am a bad mother? You know I am sensitive about that. I am trying so hard.

Notice: The conversation is now about which one of you is the "good" parent rather than who is taking the kids to baseball.

2. I want to have Christmas dinner at your house.

- Them: What kind of daughter are you? We do it at your house every year, and our mother is getting older by the day. I can't believe you are being so selfish and breaking tradition.
- You: What kind of daughter am I? I am the daughter that has been working my butt off for this family every year, and I am no longer willing to do all the work during the holidays. It isn't fair. Why do you always get to tell me what I should be doing for mom?
- Notice: The conversation is now about whether or not you are a good daughter rather than where Christmas will be spent this year.

3. I want to come up with a schedule for the project.

- Them: Gosh, I have just been so busy and then this happened and then this happened and then this happened, etc. Or, No one told me I was in charge of that!? Why didn't Amy handle it?
- You: Gosh I am so sorry all that has been going on. Do you need to talk about it? (This is a nice response, unless there is a pattern of them playing the victim. Everyone deserves a break. Everyone has bad days. If they only seem to be having bad days when they are avoiding responsibility, however, that is playing the victim, and it

is manipulation. Be kind, but don't be taken advantage
of. Notice the frequency of the pattern.)

- You: Amy isn't in charge of this; her responsibilities are...
- You: You need do a better job checking your email, etc.

Notice: In this instance, you're talking about what part of the
business involve Amy's responsibilities and buying into his story that
he didn't know what his responsibilities were. Once again, we are
talking about someone who has shown a pattern of responsibility
avoidance over time, not someone new trying to figure out the
responsibilities of a new job. The *pattern* is the marked difference.

4. I want the budget sheet you promised me a week ago.

- Them: I am the only one in this office who turns anything in on time and yet you are always on my back.
  Why don't you ever come down this hard on anyone else?
- You: I come down on plenty of people. I send reminder
  emails all the time, and I am always strict on my per-
  formance reviews of our entire team.

Notice: Don't get caught up defending how well you are doing
your job rather than talking about the job they are *not* doing.

5. I want the credit card statement.

- Them: Don't you trust me? You have some serious
  issues going on that you need to work through if you
  can't trust your own spouse. Plus, I have been super
  busy taking care of everything. Maybe if you would
  step up your game around here, I would have more
  time to do you favors.
- You: Step up my game? Last week I did this, and the
  week before I did this, and when you asked me to do
  this, I did it.

Notice: In this instance, you're talking about what you do around the house rather than talking about the credit card statement.

6. I want to know when the doctor's appointment is.

- Them: You have to control everything. You are such a control freak.
- You: I am not a control freak. Why would you say that to me? You know my sister always says that to me!

Notice: In this instance, you end up defending the fact that you are not a control freak rather than finding out about the doctor's appointment.

Remember, many toxic people like to argue in such a way that engaging in a back and forth actually equates to allowing them to win. They throw out logical point after logical point in an effort to get you to see that they are right, or that your way is right but not helpful, when they don't have ears willing to hear. Your arguments are not going to work no matter how intelligent they may be, so diplomacy will not prove useful. Figure out what you want, and force the person to stay on topic.

Note: If you are struggling in these types of conversations with teens, a different strategy is likely needed. Toxic adults often act like angry teens, while teens are still learning what it means to be good humans. Teens still need to be taught what is acceptable communication and what is not. If an adult doesn't know by adulthood, he is unlikely to change.

When it comes to communicating with a toxic person, focus on what you want rather than on changing the toxic person. This point cannot be overstated. You can give the toxic person some of what he wants as well, if you so choose. But figuring out ways to say things so that the toxic person becomes a different person is like being a dog that chases his tail.

One of the best ways to get what you want is to not go through the toxic person at all. Don't argue with him to find out what your child's doctor said. Call the doctor yourself. Anytime you can use a creative solution to go around the toxic person rather than go through the toxic person, you will be better off. Spend your time thinking about creative ways to get what you want rather than creative ways to argue for what you want.

It is also helpful to know what the toxic person wants. Does he want money? Does she want to keep up her image? Does he want to feel like he is beating you at something? If you can figure out what the toxic person wants, it can help you negotiate with him or her. At this point, your mind is probably once again coming up with some version of "This is not fair." You are probably telling yourself that they never again deserve to get what they want after all you have already given them.

While this feeling may be true, it is incredibly ineffective. You can have it all, but you can't have it all at the same time. It isn't fair that when someone wrestles a crocodile, the crocodile always wins. But they do always win—especially when they can overpower you by force. The best way to win is not to wrestle with the crocodiles in the first place. The second-best way for you to win is to distract the crocodile with a bloody chicken that seems tastier than you.

If you know what a toxic person wants and can give her some of what she wants in order to be able to move on with your life, doing so is nearly always a good decision. Did I say good decision? I meant *great* decision! The best way to move forward is to actually be able to move forward.

2. NEVER SHOW EMOTION

If you have young kids, boredom is your enemy. "I'm booooored. Can I watch TV? Can I play video games? Can I go to my friend's house?" Literally, as I was writing that sentence my son said he was bored. If you are dieting, boredom is your enemy. "Hmmmmm, I'm bored. Maybe I will just eat this entire bag of chips and the carton of ice cream." If you are dealing with a toxic person, however, boredom is your friend. Being bored by their games is wonderful. Appearing bored by their games is also incredibly useful.

Emotion feeds the drama. Toxic people love saying hurtful things to you to try to make you feel upset. When a toxic person says something mean, don't rush to answer him or her immediately. Calm down and make sure you are able to say exactly what you want to say—without any emotion. Appear bored. Remember that your emotion is the toxic person's drug! People push buttons to see which buttons will make you jump. Therefore, anytime you show emotion, a toxic person knows he has some type of control over you. He is trying to draw you into the dysfunction, because if you lose your cool, he can say, "Well look, she is the crazy one!" Keep every word neutral.

One of the saddest moments of my coaching career was the moment when I looked a fifty-five-year-old woman in the face and said, "Stop telling him what you need. He doesn't care what you need." She had given this man two kids and thirty-two years of her life, and she still hoped he would care about her side of things in a way that would move him to action. Instead, her display of emotional need was seen as a vulnerability—and, therefore, a liability. Keep the emotion out and stick to the facts. Wait twenty-four hours if you need to before you reply. A toxic person will make you feel like you need to rush to reply because you owe him. A rushed reply is usually an emotional reply. Take your time, and take out any emotional words that let you know you are feeling upset, frustrated, angry, or any other similar emotions that may have been stirred up.

3. NEVER PLAY DEFENSE

Toxic people love to get you on the defense. They do this by getting you to defend your best qualities and defend yourself against lies. If they can engage you in a conversation about the lies, they can move you away from the original purpose of the conversation. As soon as you begin playing defense, you have given validity to their statements.

If someone in a straightjacket and padded cell screamed out, "The sky is falling!" you probably wouldn't walk up to him and start explaining why the sky wasn't falling. You would shake your head, mumble something about people being crazy, and move on with your life. When a toxic person says something absurd, picture them just as you would the person in the straightjacket. Just because he says it doesn't mean it is true; however, if you start defending yourself, you are giving him the impression that you just might agree with him. We only feel the need to defend ourselves against things that get under our skin, and most things only get under our skin if there is a small piece of us that believes that it is true. Or, we know it isn't true and therefore want them to know who we really are rather than accusing us of bad qualities we don't identify with.

If someone said, "You are the greatest person I know!" you wouldn't jump into defensive mode, would you? However, if someone said, "I know you have been lying about that!" you would typically jump into defensive mode because you would want to prove your honesty. Learn your trigger points so that when someone tries to push your buttons you can be prepared. Know yourself, know your truth, and don't defend it. Ever! The second a toxic person talks you into playing defense, he is in the position of power, and you are relegated to a position of weakness.

4. REALIZE THAT IT'S NEVER GOING TO BE YOUR TURN

You can be nice this time and let the toxic person have his or her way, but that doesn't mean that next time they will return the favor. Get the next favor in writing, now. If you do allow them to have their way, detach from the idea that the toxic person will allow you to have your way next time. Yes, I know they should agree to take turns, but if someone thinks it is always their turn, they also won't believe they have to take turns to begin with.

Expecting toxic people to play fair is a guaranteed path to frustration. Plus, any time you are frustrated, a toxic person is happy. They will love watching you become upset. If you agree to something, do so because you are okay with it or ready to move on from it, not because you think a toxic person will show kindness to you later on because you were agreeable in that moment.

5. FOCUS ON WINNING, NOT FIGHTING

When you're in the midst of a situation with a toxic person, it's important to be clear about what you really want out of the situation. If your goal is to beat them, show them how tough you are, or have the last word, you are just feeding into their unhealthy behavior. I can't tell you how many people get sucked into a situation out of principle or say things such as "I just can't act in integrity and let them get away with that." I have even seen people get involved in legal battles that have nothing to do with them because they had information they had gotten during the course of their relationship.

A good rule of thumb is this: "If it wasn't against your integrity or principles while you were still in the relationship, it isn't the hill you need to die on after the relationship is over." Save the integrity for yourself, and get real about the fact that someone treated you badly and you are therefore tempted to seek revenge. Being in integrity with yourself means moving on. Your brain can use this to keep you sucked into the drama and avoid letting them go. If you want to create more justice in the world, go for it. Find something to fight for that doesn't involve the toxic person you are angry with!

The sweetest revenge is creating the best version of yourself and getting as far away from the toxic person as possible. Justice is creating beauty, peace, and happiness in your own life. Playing into a life of fighting will only drain you of the energy and resources you will need to rebuild yourself. Is it fair? Gosh, no. But, if it isn't working, stop doing it. And, by the point when you begin to consider whether or not it's time to stop, you will probably have been fighting with the toxic person for a while and know that trying to prove your point doesn't work. Remember that toxic people love fighting, so continuing to argue gives them home-field advantage.

Figure out what you truly want, and focus on your objective rather than fighting out of anger or a possibility of fairness. That doesn't mean letting a toxic person have his or her way all the time! It means fighting for the things that fit into what you really want and minimizing all other communication.

6. KEEP IT SHORT AND SWEET

Yes, I said sweet! Throughout this life of yours, you will often have to take a look in the mirror and ask, "Am I proud to be the person looking back at me?" If you are regularly engaging in mudslinging, it is going to be tough to enjoy your life. Only speak words that absolutely must be spoken. Try to turn a page into a paragraph and a paragraph into a sentence. The fewer words you speak, the better. Plus, you never know who is reading your communication or whether it could show up in a court of law one day. If you need to write out what you would really like to say as a therapeutic exercise, go ahead and write it out. Just don't send that version of the email. Send the short, emotionless email that focuses on what you want and doesn't play defense.

7. KNOW WHAT THEY WILL TRY TO USE AGAINST YOU

Toxic people are, quite simply, masters at knowing what will get you to do what they want. They are willing and able to use your best qualities against you. They may appeal to your willingness to help, your loyalty, your desire to see the best in people, or your fear of failure. Prepare for them to poke at these qualities with communication intended to get you to back down from what you want and begin defending yourself instead. Or, they may play the victim and try to get you to feel sorry for them. If you start out asking for what you want and the conversation soon moves to what they want, know that you are in a toxic situation, and the other person is not playing by the same set of rules. If they are always getting their way, they are using you against yourself.

8.   PROTECT YOURSELF

Open an email from the toxic person with a friend, run your response through a helping professional, or play your most powerful fight song before you respond to communication from a toxic person. You can't control the toxic person's response, but you can do your best to create an optimal environment in which to receive their response without it upsetting you as much. Surround yourself with people, objects, sights, smells, and sounds that make you feel safe so that the toxic person will be less likely to penetrate that sense of safety when you are forced to communicate.

The way to protect yourself is NOT to tell a toxic person how much their behavior upsets you and somehow try to appeal to their sense of kindness. Keep your vulnerabilities to yourself!

9.   STARVE YOUR EGO, FEED YOUR SOUL

There is nothing fair, right, or okay about a toxic relationship. A toxic person creates his or her heaven by creating your hell. That. Is. Not. Okay. But, in dealing with toxic people, we have to do what works rather than what we *wish* would work. And, in order to be able to effectively do that, we have to feed our souls rather than our egos. Feeding our ego allows us to feel justified, to feel right, as though we've had the last word, or otherwise proven our point. It comes across as a bit angry and often smug. Feeding our soul allows us to find peace, rise above the drama, and move our lives forward. It isn't about giving in. It is about finding a way to move on. It comes across as curious and controlled.

On the outside, feeding your ego makes it appear as though you are part of the problem; feeding your soul makes it appear as though you are rising above the problem. Feed your soul.

10. DOCUMENT, DOCUMENT, DOCUMENT

Copy the boss on the email. Keep a record of the times your ex didn't show up to get the kids. Keep a record of how many times she loses her temper. This approach will help you keep events straight

124

in your head so that you don't go nuts asking yourself if a situation is really as bad as you think it is, and you *do* give yourself some protection if it ever becomes a legal dispute or a Human Resources issue. This is a pain to do, I get it. Do it anyway!

11. BRING IN BACK-UP

The more often you can bring in back-up, the better. This means bringing your sister or friend when you have to deal with your toxic mother. It means discussing something with your toxic coworker after a meeting in plain sight of others rather than discussing matters behind the closed doors of his office. It means taking a friend when you go to pick up your stuff from your ex's house so that you don't get sucked back into his promises that this time will be different. It means finding another momma to sit with at the game if your children's father is there with his new lady friend.

12. KNOW WHEN TO DROP THE HAMMER

When I was young, my father would sing a song with the lyric "Mama grab the hammer; There's a fly on baby's head." I have no idea why my father would sing this song, nor do I have any idea why this song has not come up more in my therapy sessions as an adult. The song's message could leave all of us concerned about who might be holding that hammer and how much moonshine they had had to drink when they saw the fly land on the baby. Yet, there is a lesson to be learned from its very odd message: Every problem does not require a hammer.

Far too many toxic people think every problem requires a hammer—no matter how small the problem or how delicate the situation. You know...like a fly landing on a baby. Little problem? "Bring the hammer!" Big problem? "Bring the hammer!" Any good carpenter knows that sometimes you need a hammer, and sometimes you need a screwdriver or a paintbrush. Using a hammer to fix every problem will result in a house full of holes.

125

Yet, when it comes to sticking up for ourselves against a toxic person, we usually think we need the hammer. We need to appear strong. We want to stop being a doormat. Refuse to back down. Show them who is the boss. Because aggressively toxic people are so quick to use a hammer far too often, people think sticking up for themselves means having to use as much force as toxic people use. Yet, while some problems require force, other problems require strategy. Finesse. Grace. Patience.

This is especially important to note if you feel like you are at the end of your rope after putting up with mistreatment for far too long. You think, "I'll finally use the hammer, and then things will be better." Beware that toxic people can use your own hammer against you as well. What you call "bringing down the hammer" they will call "losing it." You haven't had a voice, so you try screaming, and in response, they tell people you are crazy. A toxic person is likely to point the finger and say, "See...I told you she was the problem."

The hammer only works if the hammer actually works. The best version of the hammer is usually ultimatums you follow through on or the natural consequence of bringing in back-up. Puffing out your chest and fighting fire with fire is more than likely going to be used against you.

Navigating a relationship with a toxic person will require you to need multiple tools in your toolbox, and a hammer is rarely your best option. Start with a feather, and then move to the hammer. For example, pivot the conversation with humor if a toxic family member keeps bringing the conversation back to your faults. "Well, Mom, I'm sure everyone would love to talk about my parenting styles, but I think we should focus on getting the turkey on the table. Who is ready to eat?" or "Thanks for the insight, John. I'll jot down your thoughts and give 'em a think."

The pivot approach is helpful in group situations when people are watching and you want to get out of looking like you are the problem when a toxic person corners you. I highly recommend practicing a couple of phrases beforehand if you know you are going to have a toxic person encounter in order to have an idea of what you are going to say. This can increase your confidence before a difficult situation arises while also calming your nerves.

To be clear, there may be situations where you absolutely need the hammer. You may have to involve lawyers or your boss or some other person in power. Know when to use the hammer carefully, however, and have your documentation in order and your facts straight when you need to drop the hammer more forcefully. Otherwise, it will look as if there are two toxic people fighting rather than one person trying to defend herself against a toxic person.

Summary: Don't utter words just to speak. Speak with purpose, brevity, and the right tool. The hammer is not always the answer, and the goal is to come up with a solution rather than just try to get back at the other person. Give yourself the gift of 10 minutes and figure out how you can strengthen your communication skills and become Toxic Person Proof™.

CHAPTER 11
BOUNDARIES

"I'll huff and I'll puff and I'll blow your house down."
—The Big Bad Wolf

A book on becoming Toxic Person Proof™ would be incomplete without one of the most popular words in relationship healing: boundaries. A boundary is defined as a dividing line. Physical boundaries, such as fences separating one neighbor's yard from another neighbor's yard, are easy to see. Emotional boundaries, on the other hand, require that you separate your problems and responsibilities from other people's problems and responsibilities. This is certainly not as clear cut as is having a fence! However, we cannot become Toxic Person Proof™ if we don't learn which problems are ours to solve and which are not.

Having strong boundaries requires knowing where you start and where you end as well as where another person starts and ends. Maintaining boundaries requires that you take care of your own stuff and expect others to take care of their own stuff. Sure, we help each other, but in healthy relationships, we take turns helping each other. Sometimes it is your turn, and sometimes it is someone else's turn.

Having boundaries can also require that you stand up for yourself and say no, saving some of your time for yourself and choosing who to spend your time with.

Unfortunately, when many people think of boundaries, they often wonder, "How can I strengthen my behavior in order to change someone else's behavior?" When it comes to people who are sometimes frustrating or difficult, that approach may work, but it isn't going to change someone who has a consistent pattern of toxic behavior. Better boundaries aren't going to change another person's personality or brain structure. I've seen far too many people in controlling relationships think that if they strengthen their boundaries, they will no longer have problems within the relationship. They think that their lack of strong boundaries is the problem, when in reality the problem is that someone else's goal is to run right over those boundaries, no matter how strong they are.

Have you ever heard the story "The Three Little Pigs"?

The first little pig builds a house made out of straw, and the Big Bad Wolf blows it down. Ugh, tough day, bro. Luckily, the first pig gets away by the hair of his chinny chin chin and goes to market to chase away the fears of the day with an ice cold can of slop.

The second little pig watches this fiasco and realizes he needs to make some serious changes in his life. He imagines the wolf's breath on his face, feels shivers down his spine, and gets serious about a new plan. He knows he needs stronger boundaries, so he joins a few Facebook groups and buys a couple of books to study up on wolf disorders. The second pig saw what happened with the first pig and realized he needed something stronger than straw boundaries to help protect him from the Big Bad Wolf, so he built a house made of sticks. The boundaries the second pig sets between himself and the wolf are stronger than the boundaries the first pig set, but the Big Bad Wolf still huffs and he puffs, and he still blows that house down. In the end, the second pig really doesn't have a better day than the first pig, despite all the extra work he put in.

The third little pig knows he needs even stronger boundaries. He reads books, consults mental health professionals, and, after pouring out his heart for weeks on end, learns that his lack of boundaries comes from his Big Pig Mama. Big Pig Mama taught him that he shouldn't have boundaries because she loved him so much and wanted to save him from turning into bacon by creating a codependent relationship between her son and herself. She taught the third pig to cry "wee wee wee" and run all the way home. The third pig knows he needs big boy- I mean big *boar*- boundaries to protect himself from the Big Bad Wolf, so he buys bricks. Lots of bricks. Loads of bricks. Buckets of bricks. Hard, rectangular bricks to keep him safe. He learns exactly where to place the bricks and how to ensure that they don't have any holes in them. The third pig does not want even one puff of wolf breath to get in. Have you ever smelled wolf breath? It's not the aroma the third pig is going for in his freshly built brick palace.

The third pig huffs and he puffs and he lays those boundaries down. He builds his brick house, stands with his hands on his hips in super pig pose, and screams, "I am strong! I know who I am! I've recovered from my Big Pig Mama drama and now I'm a bigger, badder version of swine! See me, Wolfie? See how this porker has changed for the better!"

The Big Bad Wolf is strolling down the path and the smell of sweaty swine fills his nostrils. He grins and snarls, "Showtime! This means DINNER!" The Big Bad Wolf huffs and he puffs, but despite his best efforts, he can't blow this super swine's brick house down. The third pig is thrilled. He blares the victory song "Chunky, Chunky Champions" through his living room's surround sound speakers and takes a victory lap.

YOUR BOUNDARIES WERE NOT THE PROBLEM

Have you ever been made to feel as though your boundaries were the problem rather than the toxic behavior? If you are screaming a big fat YES right now, never forget that while the three little pigs all had different boundaries, not one of them was able to change the wolf. If someone says, "You teach people how to treat you," remind them of this message. A quick retort of "Three pigs built three houses. One made of straw, one of sticks, and one of bricks. The third pig did a better job of protecting himself, but the Big Bad Wolf still tried to gobble him up. The wolf was the problem...

130

not the pig's boundaries. **Better boundaries don't make better wolves: they just protect pigs**."

This example will make the other person think while giving you a chance to make your getaway! You can have different levels of strength when it comes to boundaries, but boundaries don't change wolves: they only protect pigs. The lack of building material was not the problem. The problem was that the wolf was trying to blow the house down. The solid brick boundaries didn't make the Big Bad Wolf stop blowing. The solid brick boundaries didn't make the wolf play nice. The only way the boundaries helped the situation was by protecting the pig. Don't forget that the Big Bad Wolf is the villain of the story, not the building materials of straw and bricks, and not the first two pigs!

WHEN BOUNDARIES AREN'T THE ANSWER: MORE MORALS FROM PIG-SHAPED LESSONS

The first thing people get wrong about boundaries is assuming their boundaries will be able to change toxic behavior. The second thing people get wrong about boundaries is, they think they will feel better after they set the boundary. Sometimes after setting boundaries, we feel emotions we don't expect to feel. Let us see what else we can learn from our piggy pals!

After he realizes his brick house boundaries worked beautifully, the third pig looks out his window with elation and notices that the Big Bad Wolf has walked away to find another little pig to gobble up. The Big Bad Wolf wants a pig without brick-hard boundaries. The third pig knows he should feel better, but a little piece of him feels lost. He secretly thought better boundaries would change the Big Bad Wolf. He knew he needed better boundaries; he did the work. Without realizing it, his life's purpose had become standing up to the Wolf. And he did! So why didn't he feel better?

The third pig had to admit to himself that he had worked on boundaries in hopes of changing the Big Bad Wolf, not simply protect himself. He was left wondering, "Where is my Wolfie? Where did he go? I finally stood up to him. Now we can be friends! We are on even ground now! I did all that work so that Wolfie wouldn't always win, and I thought Wolfie would finally respect me and stop trying to blow down my house." The third pig wondered why his life wasn't working. He looked up an article on healthy coping strategies and decided to reach out to the first pig and the second pig to see if they were missing the Big Bad Wolf too.

The third pig called his porker pals to ask how they were fairing with the loss of the Big Bad Wolf from their lives. He assumed they would be worse off than he was since he had been doing the hard work of learning to set boundaries while they had only built flimsy houses of straw and sticks. He was shocked to hear them answer, "We are doing great! We realized we didn't want to spend all our time figuring out how to build stronger houses. We wanted to surround ourselves with people who weren't trying to blow down our house! Life is peaceful, and things couldn't be better."

Some people spend their time figuring out how to build stronger houses. Other people build stronger lives by surrounding themselves with people who aren't trying to blow down their house. Toxic Person Proof™ people find other pigs rather than try to tame wolves.

The third pig tried to hide his shock that the first and second pigs were doing so well. He had taken pride in his boundary building, and had even been looking down on the other two pigs. Now, he wanted to find a reason to brag. "Well, did you hear that my boundaries worked, and Wolfie couldn't blow down my house?" the third pig mentioned with a smirk.

"That's great!" said the second pig. "Sounds like all your hard work paid off! You must be thrilled."

"Yeah, I guess," replied the third pig.

"Why do you sound so upset?" asked the first pig. The third pig kind of hated the first pig in that moment, as the first pig seemed especially happy. The first pig was asking questions, but he was obviously busy as he was feeding sweet slop to his little piglet while sneaking a glance at his piggie wife. The third pig kept noticing the first pig sneaking glances at his wife's great set of teats, and the third pig wanted to throw a brick at the first pig's head so his life wouldn't be so perfect. The third pig thought his years of therapy would have fixed this by now.

"Well," the third pig replied, as he thought about his magnificently strong yet very empty house, "I thought that once I stood up to Wolfie, he would stop messing with me and we could start to get along. I thought that once he knew I was strong too, he would stop playing his big bad games and we could move into a different stage of the relationship.

The first pig tried to hide the look of shock on his face upon hearing his friend's hopes. "I hate to tell you this my fat little friend, but the truth is this: the problem wasn't that your house wasn't strong enough. The problem was that you had someone trying to blow down your house."

Did you think that by standing up to the wolf, you would change the wolf? Or at least change what the wolf thought of you? Did you think that once you gained the wolf's respect, you would change the relationship with the wolf? There is a lot we can learn from pigs who realize there is no happiness found in a lifetime of fighting wolves.

"First pig, how did you find happiness? You started off with the worst house, yet you seem to have the best life," said the third pig.

"Yeah. I mean, when the wolf blew my house down, I knew I needed to make some changes. It didn't make sense to try to change wolves. It didn't make sense to try to fight wolves. I figured the best strategy was to build a life without wolves."

BETTER BOUNDARIES DON'T MAKE BETTER WOLVES

Too often in the case of boundaries, we think our lack of boundaries is the problem rather than the other person's toxic behavior. We try to get help from others, and they say, "You teach people how to treat you" or "You shouldn't have been a doormat" or "If you had been stronger, you would have had a better relationship."

Let me be crazy clear: the problem isn't your choice in building material. The problem is that someone is trying to blow down your house and eat you up. A life without a wolf trying to blow your house down is a fine life indeed. We need boundaries to protect ourselves, but better boundaries don't make better wolves. The boundaries are to protect *us*, not save the relationship. Boundaries can help you survive a relationship with a wolf, but boundaries aren't meant to help you thrive in a situation with a wolf.

A life with boundaries in place to protect you from wolves can be a great life. A life where you try to use boundaries to change wolves is a frustrating life. Boundaries are meant to protect you -not change the wolf. Not transform the wolf into a lapdog. Wolves are not lapdogs. No matter how strong your house is, you will be happier with a lapdog than a wolf.

The Big Bad Wolf wants to eat you. Boundaries protect you. They don't cause the wolf to accept defeat and declare that it's safe to open the door and invite him in for a cup of tea. They don't cause the wolf to see you as strong and open his arms wide with love and gratitude. Wolves want their way. They want to take the easy route to dinner. They want to gobble you up. The problem isn't your lack of boundaries; the problem is that you are with someone looking to blow your house down.

ARE BOUNDARIES ONLY FOR WOLVES?

Sometimes other pigs require boundaries too, because:

1. Pigs smell.
2. They track mud inside your house.

Someone doesn't have to be a wolf in order for it to make sense for you to set boundaries to protect your time and energy. Yet, you don't want to completely shut other pigs out. Pigs (and humans) are social creatures, so you need flexible boundaries such as a low fence so you can still rub noses and check out one another's tail curls every so often. If you set a boundary that the other person respects, you are dealing with another pig, and flexible boundaries are appropriate. Building huge walls is exhausting. Only use a wall when you are dealing with a wolf. Wisdom is knowing what boundaries to use when.

TIPS FOR PROTECTIVE BOUNDARIES:

1. **Don't talk about your weaknesses in front of wolves.** That means, don't share details about your past or what you are worried about unless the person you are confiding in has proven over time to be trustworthy. Wolves can use your weaknesses against you. This can show up as a coworker who uses your vulnerability for his own gain or a friend who thinks your vulnerability is an invitation for her to tell you how you should live. Save the soft stuff for safe people.

2. **Use physical space to your advantage.** If you are in a room with a wolf, try not to sit beside the wolf. If you are in a house with a wolf, try to stay in a different room.

3. **Use time to your advantage.** If you have to deal with wolves, delay your response time and shorten your exposure time. Have a reason to leave early or arrive late.

4. **Use thoughtfulness to your advantage.** Avoid having to respond to wolves on the spot. Tell them you need to think about a response and that you will get back to them. Then, when you come back to them, be clear about your own requirements.

5. **Add your own requirement when a wolf asks you to do something.** This is a tip I learned from executive leadership coach Marsha Clark. It is helpful both at work and home. Saying, "I can take over that project for you if I am able to add another person to the finance team" allows you to say yes if they say yes to you. It is also helpful at home. "I can take you and your friends to the mall if you finish cleaning your room" or "I can be in charge of the turkey this year if everyone else brings all the side dishes." This approach

allows you to say yes without taking ownership of all the work. It allows you to create a situation that is both good for the other person *and* good for you.

6. **Have a Plan B when a wolf asks you for your time or money.** That way, you will have something to say if you are not ready to just say no. For example, "I already have a busy weekend ahead," or "I already have plans after work." If they huff and they puff and they push for another time, create space by saying, "Send me your calendar, and I'll see if I can work it out."

7. **Get comfortable with the phrase "I have put a lot of thought into this, and I don't feel like that is the right decision for me at this time."** That kind of statement is harder to argue with than "Well, I don't know," "I can't do that," or other phrases that say no without saying no. It is assertive and powerful without blaming the wolf or complaining.

Summary: A life well lived is a life, not a war. Boundaries are for your protection. Boundaries are useful for survival. Use them to keep you safe. Don't use them to convince a wolf to love you. Don't employ sturdy boundaries in order to change wolves. A lack of boundaries was not the problem in the relationship; the wolf was the problem in the relationship. The wolf is the villain of the story, not the flimsy building materials.

Boundaries are great, but be clear about their purpose. Better boundaries protect you by keeping wolves away—or at least making sure they don't eat you. Better boundaries don't make better wolves. Better boundaries can protect you physically, emotionally, spiritually, and financially.

Give yourself the gift of 10 minutes and explore your personal approach to boundaries. Do you need to drop the belief that boundaries will change toxic people's personalities? Do you need to redirect your boundaries to better protect yourself rather than changing the boundaries altogether? Do you have people in your life who respect your boundaries? If they don't respect your boundaries, is it because your boundaries are not strong enough, or is it because they want to barrel over others' boundaries? Has too much of your life focus begun to involve studying boundaries?

CHAPTER 12

TRYING TO GET OTHER TO UNDERSTAND WHAT YOU HAVE BEEN THROUGH

"Stop throwing a baseball to people who don't have arms."
—Eli Wilde

"How can I get through to others so they can see the truth about the situation? Am I just not saying it the right way? Am I just not a good communicator? Why can't I get through to them?"

When we discussed how to best communicate with a toxic person earlier in the book, it became obvious that toxic people do not have ears willing to hear. However, people who have had a toxic person encounter are often most frustrated by their friends, family, and others who also do not have ears willing to hear. It is very difficult to admit that we have been fooled by charm and charisma, and often it is easier for other people to believe the toxic person rather than believe you. Sometimes, that is because we need to communicate in a different way, yet more often it is because they do not have ears willing to hear.

Chapter thirteen will discuss good communication skills and how to help people grow ears willing to hear, but first we need to get clear about the problem we are trying to solve.

If you have found yourself trying to get through to someone about a toxic person encounter or a potentially toxic person encounter, I want you to ask yourself this: Are you not saying the right words, or does the recipient not have ears willing to hear? Because if they don't have ears willing to hear, the facts don't matter, and the truth is irrelevant. Let's look at a couple of examples.

I was on a call with a woman I will call Christine. Christine was going through a difficult divorce from a toxic ex, and her former friend was now dating her estranged husband. Sounds like a recipe for a great start to a relationship, right?

"Should I warn her? I know she isn't picking up on the red flags right now." Christine asked. "I know he seems great at first, but things got really bad as our relationship went on. I know now that a great first impression followed by a big mess behind closed doors is my ex's pattern in relationships, and I'm worried about her."

I thought carefully about how to respond. "Do you think she has ears willing to hear, or do you think your ex is going to turn it around on you and make her think you are the crazy one?" I countered.

"Well, I don't think she has ears willing to hear, but gosh, I wish someone had warned me," Christine said as tears welled up in her eyes.

"Would you have believed them?" I asked.

"No…probably not. He just seemed so wonderful on the outside, and he made it seem like life with him was in color whereas life with everyone else was in black and white. Everyone else seemed less. Less wise. Less real. Less loving. Less everything. I'm guessing she probably also feels like he is more and everyone else is less. If that is what she believes right now, she definitely doesn't have ears willing to hear. But…" I could see Christine's brain struggling to come up with reason to warn her friend. "What if she gives him ten years of her life and then eventually comes to me and says, 'Why didn't you warn me?' What will I say?"

"That's easy." I answered. "Ask her 'Why didn't you come to me and ask?' You were married to him for years. Your friend obviously knows it didn't work out, and the two of you didn't just fall out of love. Yet, she never asked you what happened. She decided to completely believe his side of the story and has never once sought out your opinion, despite a history of friendship with you. If you are divorcing him, he is no longer your responsibility. If she is pursuing a relationship with him, it is her responsibility to use her resources to figure out whether or not he is a good fit for her. Yet she seems to be choosing to believe him. Why do you think that is?"

"Because she wants to believe him and doesn't want to believe me. She is swept up in her emotions and the promise of him and doesn't want to hear what I have to say. She wants to stay in her fairytale land of promises. If she hears more details about the difficulties of our marriage, I could burst her bubble."

"Exactly! It isn't your responsibility to save her by warning her. You already know she won't listen, and your ex would use your words only to make you look bad. It is her responsibility to save herself. It doesn't sound like she wants to save herself. That isn't your fault, and it isn't a problem you can solve. If she comes to you in ten years blaming you for not warning her, I would tell her it was her responsibility to ask questions to save herself. The door is open, but she has to be the one to walk through the door. You can't drag her in and make her listen. She has to have ears willing to hear, and right now she doesn't want to listen because he seems perfect for now."

Many toxic people are amazing at first impressions and impression management. They create an aura of excitement and energy around them. Far too often, people get swept up in it. Before we get too caught up in the idea that romantic toxic relationships are in a different category and somehow worse than other types of toxic person encounters, I want to remind you that toxic people are manipulative people. The same person manipulating his date is also manipulating his boss. Manipulating his broker. Manipulating his neighbors.

I saw this type of manipulation recently between two businesses. There was a huge fallout where one longtime leader turned against another longtime leader. I will call them Mr. Stable and Mr. Charming. It felt like a Wild Wild West standoff where a line was drawn in the sand that asked, "Are you on Mr. Stable's side or Mr. Charming's side?" Hundreds of people were affected, and both businesses were significantly damaged.

Mr. Charming, who originally staged the coup and spread lies, took his customers to another business just a short drive down the road. When Mr. Stable rightfully fired one of the company's employees, Mr. Charming called a board meeting, thinking that he could bring down Mr. Stable. In reality, Mr. Stable had grounds to fire Mr. Charming on several occasions during his tenure. Mr. Charming had been working behind the scenes to undermine confidence in Mr. Stable. In this particular instance of injustice, Mr. Stable's credibility and track record prevailed, yet many who never had reason to doubt Mr. Stable were still swayed by Mr. Charming's lies.

Before Mr. Charming moved on to the next business, Mr. Stable tried to warn the new business. "Can I have a conversation with you about the multiple lies we have caught Mr. Charming in?" he asked the board of the new business. "No, thank you!" they replied.

One can only imagine that the new business was thrilled to have the charismatic Mr. Charming join their ranks and overjoyed thinking about the hundreds of customers Mr. Charming promised he would bring with him. The new business was thrilled with the possibilities and promises spouting from the lips of Mr. Charming, and they didn't have ears willing to hear! It was literally the exact same scenario as the ex-wife trying to warn the new girlfriend, only this time, hundreds of people's lives ended up being affected by Mr. Charming's promises, rather than just one person getting caught up in the anticipation of a new beginning.

At first, the new business under Mr. Charming seemed to be thriving. He brought a host of customers from the old business to the new one. The new business got swept up in the excited emotion. Swept up in the movement. But toxic people can't keep up their games forever, and the ability to make a great first impression is not the same as the ability to sustain character. Within a few short years, the new business had been divided by Mr. Charming. Tenured and beloved leaders eventually resigned. The business lost over two thirds of its customers. Rather than the board finally recognizing that they had hired the wrong person and admitting they had mishandled the situation, Mr. Charming stayed, while half of the leadership team left. It was complete chaos.

This was obviously devastating for the new business, and what seemed like a dream quickly turned into a nightmare. Hundreds of customers felt shocked, cheated, betrayed, and angry. Many of the people who left Mr. Stable felt stupid for believing Mr. Charming. The people who hired Mr. Charming doubled down on their decision and continued to defend him. The people who were forced out of Mr. Charming's business went to Mr. Stable to figure out how to pick their spirits and careers back up. Mr. Stable's business began to attract longtime customers from the business where Mr. Charming now worked.

It was, in short, a mess. A mess that could have been avoided if they had heeded warnings and had ears willing to hear. The new business didn't want to hear that their new prospect actually had a Human Resources record a mile long. In some circumstances, it does not matter what facts you have. The truth is irrelevant. The person or business doesn't have ears willing to hear because your facts do not align with what they want. Let's look at some examples of how this shows up in your real life.

Your son or daughter won't listen to what a jerk their new date is because they think the other teen is cute and popular. They don't have ears willing to hear. The truth is irrelevant.

Your former mother-in-law doesn't want to hear about how irresponsible her son is because she doesn't want to blame herself for things she saw and ignored. She doesn't have ears willing to hear. The truth is irrelevant.

Your sister doesn't want to hear about how her parenting style is enabling her older son and how her lack of boundaries is causing her son to keep falling into patterns of trouble. She doesn't want to hear that she needs to stop bailing him out and start setting boundaries. She doesn't have ears willing to hear. The truth is irrelevant.

Your friend is caught up in the excitement of a new business opportunity that just seems too good to be true. You start to dig up some dirt on her new potential business partner, but she tells you that was all in the past and this time it will be different. She doesn't have ears willing to hear. The truth is irrelevant.

Your father doesn't want to hear about how his anger is affecting others. If you explain how he hurt your sister last week, he tells you to stop being so sensitive. He doesn't have ears willing to hear. The truth is irrelevant.

Let's go back to Christine. At first, Christine came to me to figure out what specific words she could say to get through to her ex-husband's new girlfriend. She then came to the following conclusion: "She doesn't have ears willing to hear. She doesn't want to believe me. She wants to believe him. I get it now. The problem isn't what I am saying. It's that she doesn't want me to be right because she keeps hoping he is Mr. Right. So, the problem isn't my words. The problem is that her ears are unwilling to hear because she is emotionally connected to him being right and me being wrong."

Having someone believe you after a toxic person encounter is incredibly affirming. Having someone *not* believe you after a toxic person encounter often leaves you feeling helpless and angry. It is especially difficult when you are hoping to protect the wellbeing of another. It is tempting to just try harder and to speak your mind in a different way. Yet, I have seen people waste so much time and energy hoping people grow ears willing to hear. The first tragedy is that people won't listen. The next tragedy is that people waste their lives being frustrated by people unwilling to listen.

One of my core truths to live by is this: If it doesn't work, stop doing it.

Sometimes you need better words. Other times, the words you are saying are not the problem. You might be speaking to someone who doesn't have ears willing to hear, because they are emotionally connected to the truth that is convenient rather than able to see the facts you are giving them. Recognize what problem you are trying to solve so that you don't waste your life being frustrated. If you want to have more time, energy, and happiness, look for people who have ears willing to hear and save your words for them. Save your energy for building a life surrounded by people who have ears willing to hear. In the next chapter we will discuss how to help people grow ears willing to hear, but start by surrounding yourself with people who already have ears willing to hear. This will help build your confidence as you try to change the minds of others who currently do not have ears willing to hear.

Summary: Many times, it isn't what you say that's the problem. The problem is who you are saying it to. If you want to become Toxic Person Proof™, you will need to save your energy for problems that have solutions. If someone does not have ears willing to hear, forgive yourself and recognize that the issue may not have been your poor communication.

Give yourself the gift of 10 minutes and reflect on who in your life has ears willing to hear and who does not.

CHAPTER 13

HELPING PEOPLE GROW EARS WILLING TO HEAR

"I believe that people make their own luck by great preparation and good strategy."

—Jack Canfield

"But Sarah...I really need them to have ears willing to hear. I really want them to have ears willing to hear. This person is important to me, and I need her to understand what I am saying!"

If a person isn't toxic, pathological, or mentally ill, there are some techniques you can use to help him or her grow ears willing to hear. The less emotionally connected someone is to the toxic person, the easier they will be to convince. The more emotionally connected to a toxic person, the harder they will be to convince. For example, it is easier to convince a coworker that someone is toxic if that coworker was not the one who hired them. If they hired the person, they are likely emotionally invested in having been "right" and will not want to admit that they missed something in the interview. Likewise, it is easier to convince someone that their distant cousin is toxic rather than convince someone that their adult child may be toxic. Helping people grow ears willing to hear is a difficult task, but here are some communication strategies that will help.

Avoid Extreme Language and Labels

The biggest mistake I see people make when trying to get through to others is using extreme language and labels. You may have extensively researched personality disorders and mental disorders, but leading with "I think she may be a sociopath!" is probably not the best way to get someone to grow ears willing to hear!

In his fabulous book, *The Five Types Of People Who Will Ruin Your Life,* Bill Eddy tells us to describe toxic people as "high-conflict personalities" and then list three examples with supporting details. If someone has a high-conflict personality, he will have his own data to help connect the dots. If you utter the words "narcissist," "bipolar," "borderline personality disorder," or "abusive," the average individual will not have enough data to connect your words to their personal impression of the person. Using a clarifying phrase such as "high-conflict personality" will help.

Another option is describing someone as having a responsibility-avoidant personality and then providing examples. This is useful if the person about whom you're speaking fits into the victim category and is manipulating you by expecting you to take responsibility for her problems.

Whatever you do, avoid coming across as an "emotional expert." An emotional expert is deeply angry because she has been tricked for years and finally figured out what is happening. She is ready to tell her friends, family, pastors, and coworkers all about narcissism and how she has had a toxic person encounter with a narcissist. She has books! She has examples! She has finally realized that she has been manipulated/abused/tricked, and she has the authors and bloggers and YouTubers to prove it. Every time she talks about it, she gets mad and goes back to posting Facebook memes describing toxic people's behavior. She hopes sharing the memes will help her friends and family see the truth as well.

This may be one of the times you feel a bit triggered while reading. When I speak about the emotional expert, I recognize and empathize with how difficult a stage of life this is to live in. I recognize how powerful it feels to believe that your past has finally been explained, and I understand how important it is for others to comprehend what you now comprehend. However, I also understand how easy it is for a toxic person to make an emotional expert look crazy. If others do not have ears willing to hear, they cannot grow ears willing to hear by seeing how upset you are. It isn't fair, however, my goal is to help you figure out what works, not what you wish would work. The following strategies will help much more than random Facebook memes.

POINT OUT DATA PATTERNS

Whenever possible, lead with data and point out patterns. Connect the dots for people. In Chapter 12, we discussed the story of Mr. Charming and Mr. Stable. If Mr. Charming were going to be hired at a new business and Mr. Stable wanted to warn business number three, he could have connected the dots by showing a pattern of destruction.

You can also point out patterns of cheating or lying, patterns of angry outbursts, patterns with legal issues or lawsuits, patterns of being unable to hold employment, or patterns of irresponsibility. **If you are trying to help someone grow ears willing to hear, focus on pointing out examples of what someone did rather than how you felt about what they did.**

If you have a friend or family member who is trying to decide whether they are having a toxic person encounter, you can help them see patterns as well. As they talk, try to be a good listener, collect data, and later, show the person on a calendar how many days they were miserable during the previous month. You can also use the calendar technique to get clarity about the effects of your own toxic person encounter. Seeing a calendar and realizing you were miserable, fighting, being yelled at, or confused twenty-six days out of thirty during the last month is quite clarifying. Focusing on the data gets the focus off of the feelings.

PRETEND YOU ARE TALKING ABOUT SOMEONE ELSE

A great way to help other people grow ears willing to hear is to talk about their situation as if you were talking about someone else. Find songs, television shows, or news stories that sound like their situation. Or, describe their situation back to them as if it were happening to someone else. For example, "Did you hear about our friend John from high school? He left his wife for some young girl, but she ended up destroying him. There were a lot of signs at the beginning. She couldn't hold down a job, she didn't have any contact with her kids, and her ex said she was crazy. Unfortunately for John, she was also cute. I feel so sorry for him. His kids won't even talk to him anymore, and the new girl is incredibly unstable."

Obviously, you can't make up stories about mutual friends, but you can point out stories from friends or book characters that parallel their toxic person situation. What's most important is that you bring what is actually happening into the light without it coming across that you are positioning yourself as being the expert of their life. No one wants someone to tell them how they should live or tell them they are making a mistake. Try to drop breadcrumbs by pointing out other people's mistakes— people who just happen to be making the same mistakes as the friend you are talking to!

FEED THEIR WORDS BACK TO THEM

"Do you remember when you told me...?"

"Do you remember when I was going through something like this and you warned me about...?"

"Do you remember when you said...?"

"This reminds me of the time you warned me about..."

It's hard for someone to argue against their own words. Reminding them about a time when they were right creates a more powerful connection than pointing out the fact that they are now wrong.

If they go into something along the lines of "Well, back then it was different because of X, Y, or Z," you can then remind them that you thought your situation was different too. Connect with them and let them know that they are feeling exactly the way you felt. However, they were right then, and maybe (just maybe!) you are right now. Using their words, a soft tone, and tons of empathy will go far in helping them grow ears willing to hear. Positioning *them* as an expert and applying their words back to them will be much more powerful than swooping in as the expert.

GIVE THEIR SUBCONSCIOUS ABSURDITY BACK TO THEM

This approach is a bit advanced, so please be careful when using it! One of the best strategies to get someone to grow ears willing to hear involves using reverse psychology. Tell them what they want to hear or tell them what they are thinking but not saying. If someone is on the defense because she thinks you are going to disagree with her, try telling her what she wants to hear! We all have thoughts that make sense in the dark places of our mind but sound ridiculous when we say them out loud. When you bring up those thoughts and say them out loud, the person you are speaking with will often tell you why that thought doesn't make sense. However, you can compassionately remind them that it was likely the thought they had to start with!

For example, If you have a close relationship with someone you're helping, consider the following approach. Once again, use this approach with caution. This is more advanced, and this method is *not* to be used with violent toxic people. They could get very angry. Proceed with caution, and if this method doesn't feel like a fit for your situation, skip over this suggestion.

"I'm sure it will turn out fine! History hardly ever repeats itself."

"If there has been a pattern of constant problems for the last fifteen years, I think it's statistically probable that year sixteen will be a complete turnaround."

"He is probably just immature. I don't think it's really THAT bad of a sign that we are describing a forty-two-year-old man as immature? Do you?"

"That red flag probably won't be an issue later. It's absolutely worth the risk."

"How many relationships/jobs etc. have they had? Oh, I am sure this time will be different!"

"What? No healthy friendships or family relationships to speak of? Probably not a problem! All she needs is love!"

"How long was he in prison? He needs a great gal like you to show him what real love is!"

"No job? No problem! Maybe you should let him move in with you so you don't have to be alone. It will work itself out later!"

"I see no reason to set consequences with your adult children. Your son seems to be going through his fifteenth hard time in the last three weeks. I think the best course of action is whatever feels easiest for you. Setting boundaries is a pain, and I know you don't like to make him mad. I would just make sure he likes you. Producing contributing members of society is overrated anyway!"

"I'm sure that the fact that she seems unstable now is because she is lonely. You should impregnate her so she can keep herself busy caring for your DNA. That should even out her emotions. Plus, having a baby is what happily-ever-afters are made of."

"Of course it will get better after you get married!"

"That employee does seem to be too good to be true! Why bother with a background check?!"

To be fair, I did warn you that this book might make you mad. If it seems unkind to say these kinds of things to someone else, please realize how likely it is that they are telling themselves these very same thoughts. It would not bother them if the thoughts weren't ridiculous to begin with. It seems taboo to speak these kinds of thoughts out loud, but keeping them a secret doesn't mean that ridiculous thoughts aren't still running our lives. When we bring them out of the dark into the light and say them out loud, they aren't as powerful, and we can see how dangerous they can be.

We all want to Google a list of red flags and forget to Google the lies we tell ourselves that allow us to ignore the red flags.

Do You Have Ears Willing to Hear?

We can get really fired up about protecting other people through our warnings, yet we seem resistant to other people warning us. Reading the previous strategies for helping other people grow ears willing to hear has probably connected you to the difficulty of talking people into keeping themselves safe from toxic person encounters. My question to you is this: Will you have ears willing to hear in order to keep yourself safe?

Learning to Protect Yourself

As you might imagine, because of my experience in this field, people are very excited to have me around the new people in their lives to see what I pick up on about the new acquaintance. Or at least, they *think* they are excited to see what I pick up on. What they really want is for me to agree with the opinion they have already formed. "Do you think I should go into business with her? Do you think I should date him? Do you think she is who she says she is?"

When I don't pick up on anything and am able to tell someone what he wants to hear, he thinks I'm one wise cat. If I reply back with an answer that affirms what he wants to hear, such as "Your new partners seem like they would like deep conversations and intellectualizing. Is that how they prove to be when you get to know them?" People say, "Yes! Oh, you are so smart! That's exactly how they are. How did you pick up on that?"

People are very happy with me when I tell them what they want to hear. And, in many circumstances, it is safe to tell them what they want to hear because my spidey sense isn't screaming TOXIC! It is a relief not to pick up on any red flags and be able to honestly say, "Looks like a green light from me!" It's not as fun when I do pick up on red flags, points of concern, or a lack of congruence between their first impression and their past stories. Unfortunately, when people ask your opinion on whether or not someone is toxic, they do not really want your true opinion. They want their own opinion to be confirmed.

One of the biggest blind spots we have is wanting other people to have ears willing to hear and then hiding our own ears from the truth. Yet, this is how we become Toxic Person Proof™. I was leading a workshop wherein person after person was saying, "I tried to warn them, but they didn't listen!" I heard story after story and pattern after pattern of "I could have helped them! They didn't have ears willing to hear, and it's going to ruin their life!" These people were not over-exaggerating their expertise. They really did have information the other person needed. They really did have information that could protect others. Yet they could not get the other person to grow ears willing to hear, no matter how helpful the information was. The people within the workshop were very upset. The comments were flying! The emotion was building! The stories were growing! They were all in agreement that "these people should listen to us!"

And then I asked, "Are you willing to commit today to having ears willing to hear when the situation is reversed and someone is trying to warn you?"

It was like a balloon deflated. Not one person was willing to publicly state in writing that they would commit to having ears willing to hear the truth from others in the future. Researching toxic people is easy. Researching red flags is easy. Joining a support group for toxic people is easy. Reading this book is easy. Holding yourself accountable isn't always easy. There is a big difference between researching dieting strategies and passing up on the carbs at dinner.

Being Toxic Person Proof™ is about integrity and commitment. It's about being loyal to seeing the patterns in people more than the potential in people. It is seeing what *is* rather than what you wish would be. Commit to having ears willing to hear. You can get multiple opinions, but if everyone is saying the same thing, you should probably listen. Develop ears that are willing to hear!

Summary: Helping people develop ears willing to hear requires a different skill set than simply saying the same things over and over. Avoid using extreme language and coming across as an emotional expert. Point out data patterns and help others grow ears willing to hear by telling them their story as if it were happening to someone else. It is also important to have ears willing to hear in your own life on your journey to become Toxic Person Proof™.

Give yourself the gift of ten minutes and reflect on which strategy you can use to help others in your life grow ears willing to hear. Also, get honest with yourself and ask if you are willing to hear when others warn you.

CHAPTER 14

MOVING INTO ACCEPTANCE OR WHY CAN'T THINGS BE DIFFERENT

"Understanding is the first step to acceptance, and only with acceptance can there be recovery."
—J.K. Rowling, Harry Potter and the Goblet of Fire

I can already hear you saying, "But Sarah...you have no idea how badly I want them to change. I mean I really, really, really love them. I really do. They could be so amazing if they would just... My life could be so amazing if they could just... Their behavior is completely irrational. It doesn't make sense! If they could just see the light and act like a normal human and learn to function within the rules of society, things could be so much better."

Recently, I was going over spelling words with my daughter. She is great at spelling but tends to be a bit of perfectionist, so sometimes homework can be a challenge. This day was a day of challenge.

Me: Okay, now spell muffin.

Her: M-U-F-F-E-N

Me: No, it's muffin. Think about the lyric "Yes *I* Know the Muffin Man". Sing it to yourself during your test, and you'll be able to remember to spell it with the "i" rather than the "e." (At this point in the conversation, I was thinking I was quite smart and that my daughter is lucky to have a mother so creative at learning mnemonics.)

My daughter: The muffin man isn't real. So I don't actually know the muffin man.

Me: (Feeling less impressed with myself) Yeah, but I know you'll remember to use the "i" instead of an "e," right? Spell muffin.

Her: I think you're saying it wrong, Mom. My teacher pronounces it muffehn. So it should be spelled with an E.

Me: It's NOT spelled with an e.

Her: Well, it should be.

Me: *#%&*$^&*. Okay...let's try it again. How do you spell muffin?

Her: The way you say it or the way my teacher does?

They say the English language is the most difficult language to learn because it doesn't make sense. Why do we need the words are and our? Why do we need both cell and sell? Most of the time, life doesn't make sense either. Why can't people treat one another well, behave kindly, do no harm, and take care of one another? Why do we have toxic people in the first place? Why don't people get the help they need? Why do bad things happen to good people? Why do bad people get away with things? Why do scary childhoods often create scary adults? Why do people hurt those they say they love? Why would you ever play games with someone who was so desperately trying to love you? Why won't you change?

Why can't things be different?

We spend a lot of time fighting reality. We want things to be different, so we wrestle with why they SHOULD be different rather than work with the way things are. My daughter was perfectly capable of realizing that muffin is spelled with an "I" instead of an "e." But, she *wanted* muffin to be spelled with an "e" because that made more sense from her perspective. She wanted to talk about why she shouldn't have to spell it with an "i." She got mad. She used logic. She talked about how her teacher pronounced the word. She called the English language stupid. But she didn't change how we spell muffin. She didn't change anything. She just got mad.

Acceptance of reality is a tricky thing. We somehow think if we can argue with reality long enough, we can win. The Jewish Torah tells the story of a man named Jacob wrestling with God. I can relate with Jacob more than I can with any other religious figure. In the story, Jacob leaves his two wives, eleven sons, and one daughter; crosses a stream; and wrestles with a stranger until daybreak. Jacob is apparently quite the wrestler because the stranger "could not overpower him." After the struggle, the angel said, "Your name will no longer be Jacob, but Israel, because you have struggled with God and with humans and have overcome."

My guess is, Jacob had a lot of practice getting into fights and breaking them up because he had TWO WIVES. Living in an actual version of "Real Housewives of Jerusalem- The Sister Wife Edition" probably meant he'd gotten pretty good at conflict management, not to mention navigating the testosterone levels of eleven sons. But, I understand Jacob. I understand the feeling of wanting to wrestle God. I understand wanting to fight reality. I understand bargaining and begging the Universe to *change* reality so I don't have to *accept* reality.

I didn't want to become Toxic Person Proof™. I wanted toxic people not to exist.

I wanted to just be nice and let it all work out. I wanted to be kind without having to be wise. I didn't want to have to watch what I said or trust my intuition. I didn't want to have to rebuild my life. I didn't want to have to start over. I didn't want to have to stand up to people I had respected in the past. I didn't want to see pattern after pattern of bad behavior. I didn't want to put my truth against versions of other people's truth. I didn't want to think so hard about things that seemed easier for other people. I didn't want to try this hard at relationships and still have to admit defeat. I didn't want to walk away from my so-called security and walk straight into the embrace of failure.

But life wasn't asking me what I wanted. Life was asking me to take off the blinders and see the truth. Hoping reality goes away is as futile as thinking your frustration will change the way the word muffin is spelled. We can spend an infinite amount of time arguing what should be. How things should work out. How people should behave. How people should stand up for us. How the systems should change. How joint therapy should work. How the past should not affect the future.

But life doesn't work that way. Life gets to hand out the cards, and you get to figure out how to win with the hand you are dealt. Toxic person encounters are not fair. Manipulation is not fair. Control is not fair. Other people pretending they don't see bad behavior isn't fair. Giving your best to someone and having them tell you it still isn't good enough isn't fair.

We can refuse to accept reality, but we cannot refuse the results of reality. Hoping a crocodile will change into a bunny if you wait around long enough won't make its razor-sharp teeth go away. Putting lipstick on a pig won't make the pig smell any less like a pig. Telling yourself things are fine when they aren't won't make problems go away. My dad always said, "You can choose your choices, but you can't choose your consequences." Choosing to push away the truth won't change your truth.

Why do we have such a difficult time accepting reality? Accepting that someone is toxic sucks. One of the main reasons we turn to smart-girl/guy syndrome is because accepting that a toxic person isn't going to change no matter how hard we work feels horrible. We feel helpless and hopeless when we realize we can never be good enough to change someone. We feel like there is power in working harder. We don't feel powerful giving up.

How Would You Change Autism?

I want you to imagine that you have an autistic child. I have been around children with special needs since I was in kindergarten, thought of becoming a special needs teacher, and have a first cousin with special needs. Please know I have incredible compassion for this situation and a great understanding of the difficulties faced when having the honor and added responsibility of caring for someone with special needs. Please see my heart, and know I am not trying to insult people with special needs. I am simply trying to make a point to help others become Toxic Person Proof™.

Imagine parents who are looking to find a teacher to help make their child no longer autistic. Imagine them getting angry with the teacher for the fact that their child is still autistic after spending a year with that teacher. Imagine the parents screaming at the teacher for not doing a good enough job. Imagine the parents saying, "If you had been a better teacher, my child wouldn't act that way! If you had been more attentive, my child would have developed a different brain structure!" Now imagine the parents dragging their child to doctor after doctor expecting to find the cure for autism and being mad that the doctors couldn't cure it.

Now let's look at your own life. I want you to imagine finding the "right" therapist to cure autism. I want you to imagine trying to be sexier to cure autism. I want you to imagine trying to have better boundaries to cure autism. I want you to imagine thinking that if you are the perfect employee, you can cure autism. I want you to imagine being more forgiving to cure autism.

In a fabulous conversation I had with Sandra L. Brown, M.A. from The Institute, she described pathology as being a "psychological cousin" to autism. Personality disorders are not merely mental health issues. Sandra shared that research now shows that personality disorders have neurobiological differences that can be seen on MRI brain scans. That means there are neuro differences between those with personality pathology and those without, making personality disorders just as neuro-oriented as they are mental health issues. Further, someone's brain is not something an employer, Human Resources department, lawyer, or devoted wife can do anything about. I will never forget Sandra asking me, "Can you have such great boundaries that you turn brown eyes blue? Can you be so kind, so understanding, so devoted, so hard working that you can change the color of someone's eyes?"

Smart-girls/guys tell themselves they can do anything. They tell themselves that with enough hard work, enough practice, enough love, enough grit, enough care, they can do anything they set their minds to. However, even smart-girls/guys are unlikely to believe that they can work hard enough to turn brown eyes blue. They are unlikely to believe they can be so strong, so understanding, so wonderful that they can cure autism. They recognize that hard work and good communication have their limits. Applying those limits to toxic people will serve you well. And recognizing that you cannot be so amazing that you can change someone's personality any more than you can change the color of someone's eyes keeps you safe from having smart-girl/guy syndrome used against you.

Maybe I Can Be Amazing Enough to Change Them

Smart-girls/guys are so good at earning their place in this world. They are good at earning a seat at the table, earning a trophy, earning a gold star from the teacher. Yet, the blind spot of smart-girl/guy syndrome is this: **You cannot be so amazing that you change someone else's personality.** They act that way because of who *they* are, not because of who *you* are. They are angry because they use their anger to get their way, not because your actions are always making them angry. They are abusing drugs and/or alcohol because they are using them as a way to cope with their life, not because you are supposed to be solving all their problems for them. It isn't your job to make sure they don't have any problems to cope with. They are jerks to their coworkers because they can get out of work duties, not because the coworkers aren't working hard enough.

Despite what the toxic person may have told you, you cannot be so awful that you change a person's personality and brain structure. You cannot be so amazing that you can change a person's personality and brain structure either.

I will never forget when I found out that someone had cheated on Beyonce. Beyonce for crying out loud! Was she not sexy enough? Not connected with her power enough? Not successful enough? Of course not. The person who cheated on Beyonce cheated on Beyonce because of his choices and his personality, not because of Beyonce's shortcomings. She could not be so rich, so talented, so beautiful, or so perfect that she earned his fidelity. If she judged herself on her ability to keep her man from straying, her report card would have a big fat F. Yet she is absolutely amazing in so many ways. Is it fair to put her in the category of failure? I certainly don't think so.

Further, I don't think it's fair to categorize plenty of other amazing people as failures. If you're one of the amazing people out there who got a bad case of smart-girl/guy syndrome and thought you could be so amazing as to transform someone else's personality, chisel down their selfishness, calm their temper, heal their wounds, stop their cheating, or get them to live up to the potential, please know that their behavior was not your fault. You cannot be so amazing that you change someone else's personality. It's like trying to be so amazing that you change the color of their eyes. When we are talking about an adult, it's important to acknowledge that their genetic predisposition, their personality, their brain, and their way of life have been that way for a long time.

I'm going to say it again louder for the people in the back. **If a toxic person does not change who they are to be who you want them to be, it doesn't mean something is wrong with you! You cannot be so amazing that you are able to change another's personality!**

Cheating isn't the only toxic person problem, but I think the case of Beyonce drives home this point. If Beyonce wasn't amazing enough to change a cheater's personality, then you aren't amazing enough. If Eva Longoria, Halle Berry, Kim Kardashian, Sandra Bullock, Shania Twain, Christie Brinkley, and Elizabeth Hurley weren't amazing enough to prevent their men from cheating, I feel like it might be time to go easy on yourself. Your looks, your personality, and your lack of being amazing wasn't the problem. The fact that the other person wanted to cheat was the problem. And cheating isn't the only toxic person problem. People love based on who they are, not who they are with.

Let's also look at how amazing one would have to be to become Great Britain's prime minister. Just before the brilliant Winston Churchill and the iron strength of Margaret Thatcher, Neville Chamberlain was one of the few world leaders to sit down with Adolf Hitler. The most powerful man in Britain would have had above-average intelligence. Yet, after meeting Hitler three times and spending several hours together, Chamberlain is quoted as saying that Hitler showed "no signs of insanity but much excitement." It has gone down in history as one of the biggest mistakes of all time, however it is unfair to place all the blame on Chamberlain. He was far from the only person who misread Hitler. He simply believed in the general good of people. He also believed in his ability to negotiate with foreign leaders. Still, he could not be so amazing as to be able to change Hitler's personality or pathology.

Maybe It Really Is My Fault

The super tricky thing about smart-girl/guy syndrome is that we WANT it to be our fault. After all, if it is our fault, we can fix it. If it is our fault, we are in control. If it is our fault, we can make it better. We can make ourselves better! We WANT to be able to do something to change the situation. Accepting that we can't change another person makes us feel powerless. We have to admit that we are not the great and powerful Wizard of Oz. We are not a magic fairy godmother. We are not Cupid. We are not the ruler of the world. We are not the King of everything. And that is scary, because that means we have to move into acceptance.

"How I wish this was my fault. That I could just work harder and make changes in myself. Maybe I could fix it.

But, when it's them that choose to destroy and discard, there is nothing I can do.

I'm helpless like a bystander watching a train wreck with everything I hold dear inside.

I tearfully gather up all my best pieces from the wreckage and clutch them dearly to my heart like a protective mother.

Walking away from the wreck I realize even though painful, I am free.

Now it's on me.

Now it's my choice.

How I move forward and the choices I make are in my power.

I get to choose if I dwell on the wreck or not.

I still have all the best pieces of me". - Detra Borner

Summary: Acceptance is hard. But continuing a toxic person encounter and hoping brown eyes turn to blue is harder. You cannot change another person, but that doesn't mean that you cannot change your own life. There is literally no hope of changing someone's brain structure. There is, however, all kinds of hope for learning how to take back your thinking, regain your confidence, live in clarity, and find peace.

The next time you find yourself saying, "It shouldn't be this way!" ask yourself, "How will I ensure I'm Toxic Person Proof™ in the future?"

CHAPTER 15
LEARNING TO GIVE YOURSELF PERMISSION

"Learn to value yourself, which means: fight for your happiness."

—Ayn Rand

My mother always told me I shouldn't wear yellow. My mother's mother also told me I shouldn't wear yellow. I learned other important lessons as a child. Lessons like, don't spend everything you make, don't drink milk out of the carton, and don't fight with your sister. But the lesson that really sticks out is the one that told me I shouldn't wear yellow. My home economics teacher agreed with the other matriarchs in my life. When I wasn't learning how to make lasagna or sew together my own boxer shorts, I was learning what colors went with my hair, which was very dark and my skin, which was very white. Apparently, I am what you would call a "winter." Because I was a winter, I should stick to jewel tones. Royal blue? Yes, please. Deep purple? Sounds great. Red? Don't mind if I do.

But, yellow? No. Never, ever yellow. (My mother has since taken back her statements regarding the color yellow, and we have been able to live happily ever after. Love you, Mom!)

Fast forward twenty years (and the rise in popularity of spray tans), and one day I reached my breaking point. I wanted to go savage. I wanted to get crazy. I wanted to throw caution to the wind, spread my wings, and finally learn to fly with the eagles. So I bought a yellow shirt.

Okay...one might call it gold. And, at this point, I had upgraded my skin tone from Frosty to Fergie. But still, it was pretty much yellow. And I was wearing it. I cranked up "Born To Be Wild" and walked out of my house, wondering if the gods of fashion would send down lightning bolts to punish me for my sins.

All day, I got...compliments. In fact, I got lots of compliments. "I love that color on you," "Wow! That's a great color for you," and "I have never seen you wear that color. Yellow is definitely your best color."

What? Could it be true? Could I have spent years and years asking other people what was best for me instead of trying it on myself? In a word: abso-freaking-lutely. I bet you have done this too. I bet you have had a delectable closet of choices in front of you, and I bet you got nervous and asked other people's opinions. I bet you have held things up to the mirror of your own life, seen it with your own eyes, and immediately turned to someone next to you and asked, "What do you think of this? Is this a yes or a no for me?"

While we all need feedback from others to grow into our best selves, many of us are way out of balance. We don't know ourselves terribly well, so we ask others for permission to live our lives. **Problems come when we assume that everyone else's ideas for our lives are better than our own. Problems come when we assume that everyone else's thoughts of our choices are more important than our own.**

Problems arise when we feel like we have to ask other people for permission to live our own lives. When we can't figure out what to believe, we run to ask someone else what they think. When we can't figure out which direction to go, we ask someone else for the directions to our own life. When we can't figure out our own right or wrong, we keep going to the mirror, looking at ourselves, and then turning away from ourselves. We turn around, look at others, and ask, "What do *you* think?" instead of asking ourselves, "What do *I* think?"

Enter the toxic person. Enter mother knows best. Enter Mr. ALWAYS right. Enter the unhealthy religious community. Enter the boss getting you to take the hits so he can take the glory. "I know what you should do. I know what is best for you. I know who you should be. I know what you should think. I know what you should believe. I know you better than you know yourself. Listen to me and you will be happy. Listen to me and we will both be happy. Listen to me and all will be well. Listen to me, listen to me, listen to me."

Toxic people want you to listen to them instead of to the inner voice within yourself in order to know what is true. Toxic people want their voice to be the loudest voice in your life. Toxic people want their needs to be the biggest priorities in your life. Toxic people want your energy to revolve around them, and if we aren't careful, our emotions, our values, and our smart-girl/guy syndrome can convince us that this is the right thing to do.

HELPING PEOPLE BECOME MORE SELFISH IS NOT THE RIGHT THING TO DO

In an effort to break off a toxic person encounter, you often hear one line over and over: "You deserve better." While I do think people deserve better than toxic behavior, I don't see the phrase "I deserve better" aligning with too many good people. If their values include doing good for others, not being selfish, and believing in people's ability to change, then "I deserve better" rarely helps them break off a toxic person encounter.

Ask this instead: "Is your purpose on earth to help selfish people become more selfish? Is your purpose here on earth to help angry people avoid working on their anger? Is your purpose here on earth to cover for someone who is lying and cheating? Is your purpose on earth to be someone's emotional punching bag? What legacy will you leave? Will you be someone others can use? Will you be the man or woman everyone knows they can manipulate? Will you be the defender of bad behavior because you don't want to see bad behavior? Will you be the toxic person protector?"

I won't soon forget a conversation I overheard between two women at a coffee shop. One woman was concerned that her child was going to get thrown out of daycare. Apparently, the child was biting the other kids, which resulted in angry parents, a frustrated preschool director, and a mom worried about her child getting kicked out of one of the nicest preschools in the area. The mom, finally at her wit's end, had scoured the internet looking for advice on how to stop her son's enjoyment of biting and finally came to the only logical conclusion: She needed to bite her son back. This plan actually worked great! The boy immediately stopped biting and started hitting.

To be super clear, I am not saying this one-year-old is toxic and obviously doomed for life. I recognize that kids do things at the age of one that they don't do at the age of thirty. This story *does*, however, illustrate the frustration that comes about when trying to get a toxic person to change. You beg and plead for them to stop one destructive behavior and they start another destructive behavior. Healthy people grow up and mature and learn appropriate ways to interact with others. Toxic people remain tantrum-throwing toddlers, angry teens, or responsibility-avoidant fourth graders. And with toxic people, the one problem isn't *the* problem. The toxic person's character, selfishness, inability to play by the same set of rules, and/or unwillingness to do anything good for others is the issue. As soon as you fix one problem, another pops up. As soon as you fix the biting, they start hitting. As soon as you get rid of one affair, they bring in another. As soon as you set boundaries around the way they talk to you, they simply get better at their game. You work, you have meetings, you bring in outside help, and you think you have a breakthrough. You are so excited. You hope. And then...they find another way to get what they want. You fix the problem of biting, but are unable to fix the problem of aggression. Trying to get a toxic person to change is like trying to hold water in your hands. You can work and work at it, but they will always find a way to go around your boundaries, around your expectations, and around your rules.

Remember that toxic behavior is a spectrum and a pattern. The more patterns you've seen of bad behavior, the more toxic a person is. When you try to solve one problem (like the mom with her son biting) and think that will solve the problem in the relationship, you are going to see another problem pop up. It is always something with toxic people.

Become Toxic Person Proof™. Give yourself permission to use the tools from this book and apply them to your life. The fewer toxic people encounters you have, the happier you will be. The fewer toxic people problems you are solving, the more you will be able to tap into your creativity. You will have more energy and more clarity, and you won't be walking through life asking, "What the heck just happened?" Learn to know yourself, and stop talking yourself out of the flags being red. Learn what pieces can be used against you and protect yourself.

Life is good when you're Toxic Person Proof™.

REFERENCES

Preface

"Californication (TV Series 2007–2014) - IMDb." https://www.imdb.com/title/tt0904208/. Accessed 28 Oct. 2020.

Chapter 1: Getting Control Of Your Head, Your Heart And Your Life

Brown, S. L. (2005). *How to spot a dangerous man*. Alameda, CA: Hunter House Publishers.
Brown, S. L. (2018). *Women who love psychopaths*. Mask Publishing.
Simon, G. K. (2013). *Character Disturbance the phenomenon of our age*. Marion: Parkhurst Brothers.

Chapter 2: Learning to See Red Flags

"Jeffrey Epstein: Filthy Rich | Netflix Official Site." 13 May. 2020, https://www.netflix.com/title/80224905. Accessed 28 Jan. 2021.
"Mel Gibson 'caught on tape admitting he hit ex-girlfriend ....'" 8 Jul. 2010, https://www.dailymail.co.uk/tvshowbiz/article-1293077/Mel-Gibson-caught-tape-admitting-hi t-ex-girlfriend-Oksana-Grigorieva.html. Accessed 8 Dec. 2020.

"RAINN.org Perpetrators of Sexual Violence: Statistics." https://www.rainn.org/statistics/perpetrators-sexual-violence. Accessed 28 Jan. 2021.

Stout, M. (2006). *Sociopath next door.* Harmony Publishing.

"Digital therapy platform for paranoia & personality ... - X4impact." https://x4i.org/social-challenge-idea/health-and-well-being+sustainable-cities-communities/digital-therapy-platform-paranoia-personality-disorders/c-3hpn8t3qt. Accessed 28 Jan. 2021.

"NIMH » Personality Disorders." 1 Nov. 2017, https://www.nimh.nih.gov/health/statistics/personality-disorders.shtml. Accessed 28 Jan. 2021.

"Sarah K Ramsey interviews Sandra L. Brown https://www.youtube.com/watch?v=LGhvMWR2-5U

Chapter 3: Yes, Toxic People Know What They Are Doing

Simon, G. K. (2013). *Character Disturbance the phenomenon of our age.* Marion: Parkhurst Brothers.

Bancroft, L. (2008). *Why does he do that?: Inside the minds of angry and controlling men.*

Brantford, Ont.: W. Ross MacDonald School, Resource Services Library.

Chapter 4: Blindspots

"Americans are overconfident in their driving skills - Business Insider." 25 Jan. 2018, https://www.businessinsider.com/americans-are-overconfident-in-their-driving-skills-2018-1. Accessed 29 Jan. 2021.

Thomas, G. (2019). *When to walk away: Finding freedom from toxic people --study guide, six sessions.* Grand Rapids, MI: Zondervan.

Simon, G. K. (2016). *In sheeps clothing: Understanding and dealing with manipulative people.* Marion, MI: Parkhurst Brothers.

Gladwell, M. (2020). *Talking to strangers: What we should know about the people we dont know.* London: Penguin Books.

Chapter 6: Understanding Smart-Girl/Guy Syndrome

"Symptoms of Codependency - Psych Central."https://psych-central.com/lib/symptoms-of-codependency. Accessed 30 Jan. 2020.

"Do-Re-Mi Lyrics - Maria and the Children - Soundtrack Lyrics." 31 Jan. 2001, https://www.stlyrics.com/lyrics/the-soundofmusic/do-re-mi.htm. Accessed 3 Feb. 2021.

Frankl, V., & Frankl, V. (Writers). (1946). *Man in Search of Meaning.*

Chapter 7: I Need More Data

Simon, G. K. (2016). *In sheeps clothing: Understanding and dealing with manipulative people.* Marion, MI: Parkhurst Brothers.

Bancroft, L. (2008). *Why does he do that?: Inside the minds of angry and controlling men.* Brantford, Ont.: W. Ross MacDonald School, Resource Services Library.

Chapter 9: Mental Strategies To Solve When You Can't Just Walk Away

"Esther Perel: Are We Asking Too Much Of Our Spouses? : NPR." 25 Apr. 2014, https://www.npr.org/2014/04/25/301825600/are-we-asking-too-much-of-our-spouses. Accessed 3 Feb. 2020.

Reid, T. J. (2020). *The seven husbands of Evelyn Hugo: A novel.* New York: Washington Square Press.

Chapter 13: Helping People Grow Ears

Eddy, B. (2018). *The five types of people who will ruin your life.* Published by TarcherPerigee.

Chapter 14: Moving Into Acceptance Or Why Can't Things Be DIfferent

"Chamberlain's account of his first meeting with Hitler - Cabinet Office ...." http://www.nationalar- chives.gov.uk/cabinet-office-100/the-munich-pact/ chamberlains-account-of-his-first-meeting-with-hitler/. Accessed 3 Dec. 2020.

Made in United States
Orlando, FL
05 October 2023

37601666R00117